Except For One Little Problem:
Memoir of a Life in Hiding

Except For One Little Problem:
Memoir of a Life in Hiding

Joan Denson

BARRICADE
BOOKS

Fort Lee, New Jersey
www.barricadebooks.com

Published by Barricade Books Inc.
185 Bridge Plaza North
Suite 308-A
Ft. Lee, NJ 07024

Library of Congress Cataloging-in-Publication Data
Denson, Joan
        Except for one little problem : memoir of a life in hid-
        ing / Joan Denson.
            p. cm.
        ISBN: 1-56980-212-2
        1. Lesbians--United States--Biography. 2. Lesbians--
        United States--Identity. 3. Lesbianism--United States.
        HQ75.4.D46A3 2001
        305.48/9664 B 21

First Printing
Printed in Canada

Contents

Author's Note

Many names have been changed in order to respect the
privacy of the persons and places in my past.

Dedication

To all those who have marched to a different drummer.

"We dance around in a ring and suppose,
But the secret sits in the middle and knows."
—Robert Frost

1 Finding Anne Frank

"Ma! I'm going to Amsterdam! Papa Frank invited me!" I bolted into the kitchen clutching Otto Frank's letter.

Hold on, Joan. Nineteen-year-old girls don't go running off to Europe alone."

"But I've been waiting for this chance for four years!" To meet Anne Frank's father had been my dream ever since as a 15-year-old schoolgirl I'd picked up a book from a rack outside a Chicago subway that I thought would be a sexy little paperback, *The Diary of a Young Girl*. Riding home on the train I'd devoured the book, through its pages becoming one soul with Anne Frank, a girl my age who understood me as no one else could, who shared my frustrations and my longings to be someone special one day. I was certain Anne Frank and I were meant to become pen pals and best friends.

When I read on the last page, "In March 1945, Anne Frank died in the concentration camp at Bergen- Belsen," I was devastated. We would never laugh together; we would never share secrets. No one I knew in my life had died; I had just found her, and I couldn't bare it. I ran home from the station and dashed off an impassioned letter to the publisher, never imagining that they would forward it to Anne's father, the family's sole survivor. He answered my letter, and we began a faithful correspondence. Now he had invited me to see the place where Anne had lived!

"I'm sorry, it's just too dangerous. Some cab driver could slip you a Mickey and sell you into white slavery!" My mother heightened the drama of her statement by wiping away tears caused by the onion she was peeling. I hadn't a clue what "slip you a Mickey" meant: Was Mickey Mouse in Europe, too? But there was no point in asking; she'd made up her mind—that is, until Otto Frank's next letter arrived, addressed to her and my dad.

August 3, 1958

My Dear Miriam and Irving,

I have enjoyed meeting your daughter through her wonderful letters, and look forward to her upcoming trip to Amsterdam. Of course we understand your concern for Joan's well being while away from home. My wife and I promise to keep close contact with Joan throughout her journey. Feel free to contact me at any time.

Warm Regards,
Otto and Fritzie Frank

Dad laid his glasses on the table and turned to mom, "Maybe if Goldie and Hal let Suzie go, too."
"This is my trip!" I slammed the table. "I'm *not* taking Suzie!" Miriam shrugged, "Frankly, I never thought it would come to this. But, the only way I'll feel comfortable is if your uncle Hal lets Suzie go...." I tried to sound composed, but my voice climbed several registers. We're not even friends! Just because she's my cousin! It's not fair." Now everything depended on that jerk, Suzie.

***

As Suzie dragged her luggage to the holding area, I looked up at the massive ocean liner.
"Wow!" I turned to her. "Isn't it gigantic?" I craned my neck for a better view.
"Fabulous," she giggled. "Why are we standing around gaping like kids? Let's find the *Bon Voyage* party!"

With that, Suzie and I boarded the SS Princess Beatrix for Rotterdam. I hesitated before stepping onto the white gangplank. This was it. My whole body tingled. No more dreaming, no more saving every penny. I was off on the most incredible journey of my life. Almost five years had passed since I'd read *The Diary of a Young Girl* and written to Anne's father, Otto Frank.

On my own for the first time. The thought scared me. Well, I'm not really on my own. I've got Suzie. Even though she was boy crazy, Suzie actually wasn't that bad. Nothing really mattered now anyway, except getting to Amsterdam.

Suzie, however, had other goals for this trip, and it didn't take long for the guys to discover us. The first night, as we stood in line for the dining room, we heard two young men behind us whisper,

"Hey, get a load of those two!"

"Yeah, very nice. Let's find out where they're seated."

Sure enough, our table that night seated four. Our admirers marched toward us behind the maitre d'.

"Hi, I'm Bob Martelli, and this is my friend, Charles Berger. What a pleasant surprise to be seated at this table with such lovely girls!" Subtle.

Charles and Bob turned out to be older men, in their mid-20s, and from New York. Both were Rhodes scholars at Eastern universities. I'd only recently finished my sophomore year at junior college, and Suzie was a receptionist at a dentist's office. We were definitely in over our heads.

* * *

Charles and I ended up strolling the deck most evenings for the rest of the trip. Stars glistened against a black-velvet sky while music wafted up from the deck below, filling me with vague romantic longings, but not for him. I tried to imagine my Mr. Wonderful but couldn't think of anyone. It became a challenge to fend off his hands.

"Joan," he pressed against me, "you don't know what

you're missing. Honey, I have a once-in-a-lifetime treasure to show you. Come to my cabin."

I thought he might be talking dirty, but I wasn't sure. Meanwhile, my voluptuous sidekick had landed a young Dutch officer and thereafter returned to our cabin in the wee hours of every morning. (Except for Doris Day, I must have been the only real virgin of the 1950s.)

At the farewell dinner, my injured suitor inscribed our group photo: *Dear Joan, Thanks for the wild time in Cabin 404. You have a great body. I'll always remember you. Charlie.* I winced. What decent girl owned a photo like that? I reluctantly tossed my tainted souvenir into the ocean.

***

After all the passionate letters I'd exchanged with Papa Frank telling him of my hopes and dreams, we were finally going to meet. It was really happening. Would he see Anne in me? I couldn't wait to feel Anne's presence everywhere.

In Amsterdam, I walked into the hotel that Papa Frank had carefully pronounced over the phone, insisting I repeat it back until he felt sure I'd find it. Anxious now, I searched the faces of the people in the lobby. Would I recognize him? Suddenly, I knew that face, so like Anne's. Papa Frank sat alone on a divan. Seeing me, he stood and I ran into his outstretched arms. He clasped my hands as he stepped back to look at me. He was tall and aristocratic, with a surprising softness in his eyes.

"Joan, it's so good to meet you after all the letters and the many years." Gracious and distinguished, he seemed to have stepped out of a bygone era.

"Papa Frank, I want to see everything connected with Anne's life. Would that be hard for you? It's all right to tell me the truth…"

"Dear Joan, I would not have invited you if I felt it would be too painful. You are very sweet to ask."

I relaxed. I wasn't intruding. I blurted out, "You look exactly like Anne!" Papa Frank stiffened. *Leave it to me! I hurt him.*

"People used to tell Anne how much she looked like me. It's odd being known as Anne Frank's father...very hard...very strange...."

"I'm so sorry, please forgive me."

"No darling, hush, it's fine. There is nothing to forgive. I'm too sensitive about foolish things. How about some wonderful ice cream? I know you'll enjoy the sweets café Anne mentions in her diary." Papa Frank put my arm through his. I felt proud as we walked from the hotel, through narrow alleyways and up streets crowded with cars and bicycles until finally arriving at the quaint shop Anne had frequented with her friends.

While we drank chocolate sodas at a white filigree ice cream table, I imagined what it would be like to sit there and chat with Anne. She'd tell me about all the boys who craved her attention. After a while, she'd blow me a kiss, then disappear into a crowd of admirers. She was charismatic and lovely! Who wouldn't want to lose themselves in those dark, soulful eyes?

Otto Frank interrupted my reverie, "Would you like to meet Miep Gies today?"

All my fantasies were coming alive. I could barely breathe. "Yes, of course!"

Papa Frank and I walked along the canals to Miep's apartment. He rang the buzzer. "Miep, it's Otto Frank and a friend." An attractive woman of about 35 unlatched the door.

"Miep, this is Joan, my pen pal from Chicago."

"Mein Gut, Chicago," Miep chuckled, "do you know Al Capone?" She was a lovely woman filled with youthful exuberance, just as Anne had described her. Mr. Frank's Christian secretary had provided black market food that kept the group alive in hiding. After the arrest, Miep locked Anne's diary in a desk drawer, planning to keep it safe for her until the girl could return. Aware of the penalty for harboring Jews, Miep had nonetheless appeared at gestapo headquarters attempting to "buy back" her friends. The Nazis had denied her request.

"Joan is most anxious to see Anne's diary. Would you like to come along, Miep?"

"If you don't mind, no, this day is very busy." Her gray eyes searched my face, "Papa Frank tells me you love Anne, yes?" I nodded, and blushed.

***

The following day Papa Frank took me to 263 Prinsengracht, the site of the Secret Annex. Upstairs in the office, he pushed aside the fake bookcase that concealed the rooms behind, where the little group had hidden before their discovery.

Overwhelmed, I stood in Anne's bedroom examining her collection of movie stars, still pasted to the walls. Yellowed newspaper clippings of Robert Taylor and Ginger Rogers smiled out at me. My bedroom walls were plastered with movie stars too. We had so much in common. I squelched the tears forming behind my eyes.

We mounted the steps to Peter's garret, where he and Anne had enjoyed a bit of privacy for their talks and secret kisses. Through the tiny window I saw the rooftops of Amsterdam—their only glimpse of the outside world. I peered through the same garret window and wondered, will I ever feel about anyone the way she felt about Peter? I sensed Anne there, her secrets and her pain.

With a tremble in his voice, Papa Frank asked me, "Would you like to see Anne's papers?" I nodded. My eyes widened, watching him remove stacks of notebooks and sheets of papers from his large black briefcase. He handed me the small, plaid, cloth-bound diary he had given Anne for her 13th birthday.

I opened the first page. I already knew how it began: "*I don't intend to show this…notebook bearing the proud name of 'diary' to anyone, unless I find a real friend…*"

Surely, I was that real friend. Papa Frank sat next to me Indian style on the floor of the now-empty, dust-filled bedroom. I clutched the Holy Writ to my chest. This little book has known her breath, her touch. The cloth-covered diary bore the slightest scent of rose perfume. I ran my fingertips over the pages she had written, fascinated by the many sheets she'd covered with white tape, concealing nasty comments about her mother. What most surprised me were the additional black-and-white notebooks and separate sheets of papers filled with her writing that Otto pulled from his bag. He said Anne rewrote entries several times, intending to convert the manuscripts into a book after the war. I saw clearly the girl who never doubted her talent or her destiny. There on the floor with Papa Frank holding her diary, was my most intimate time with Anne. In the stillness of the room, my body felt heavy with loss. *She'll never be back.*

***

A week later, Suzie rejoined us, having caroused with her shipboard romance for the entire stay. We celebrated our last night in Amsterdam at the pre-war apartment where the Frank family lived before hiding. It was now occupied by the Vandermillers, who generously welcomed us into their home.

Kenny Mason, a husky New York exchange student, lived with the Vandermillers. He and Suzie flirted openly, though his dark, ravenous eyes were glued to my body. I looked away, but his eyes followed me. After dinner, I bolted for the balcony. He pursued, trying to engage me in conversation.

"I'm an art history major at Amsterdam University," he said. "Have you seen the Rembrandts and van Goghs? They're sensational."

"I understand the Vandermillers have given you Anne's bedroom. That must be something—to be in her bed!"

"I'd rather be in yours," he leered. "Listen, Suzie says you'll be in Paris next week. We could meet there—"

"No, I'm sorry, that's impossible. We have every second planned."

His face contorted, "Anne Frank! Anne Frank is all that's on your mind." His eyes were hot. I could feel his contempt. "You're in love with a dead girl?"

I turned and walked away, shivering with rage. How dare he smear her memory with his filthy thoughts. Suddenly I felt scared. *Was this true? Of course, I loved her... the whole world loves Anne Frank.*

Anyway, if she were alive, we wouldn't be in love. We would just be friends. Still...

I couldn't shake off his raspy voice. *Kenny's an idiot.* A girl refuses him, and he turns it into something ugly. *Forget it, he couldn't understand innocent affection, couldn't recognize platonic love if it hit him over the head.* But Kenny's accusation would force me into awareness of something I'd refused to see.

***

"Suzie! Ingrid Bergman's in Paris doing *Tea and Sympathy*, and I got us tickets for tonight!" I was rinsing out panties in the roach-infested bathroom of our Left Bank hotel room.

Suzie was sprawled on the bed, her ice-blue eyes half shut. "I'll have to pass. I have a date with a gorgeous Frenchman who just happens to speak English. You know, I've been watching you. You just don't get it, Joanie. Is there something wrong with you? People come to Paris for romance! You sure have a lot of growing up to do."

I slammed the bathroom door. I didn't want her to see the giant tears welling in my eyes.

"Come on, Joanie. I didn't mean to hurt your feelings. Why don't you come with us tonight? I'm sure he has a friend," Suzie called through the door.

I couldn't answer. She would've heard the tears I was holding back with everything I had. *Why wasn't I crazy for Frenchmen like Suzie? Or why hadn't I liked Charles Berger or Kenny Mason for that matter. Was Kenny right? Absolutely not! No one is in love with a dead person. No girl is in love with a girl. Except homos.*

Suddenly I felt nauseated. My skin crawled. Maybe I'm a

girl who loves girls. Oh God, that's the worse thought in the world. I'm going to throw up. It's repulsive to be in love with a girl. No one can know, ever. I'll get over it. I know I will. I have to.

2 Prom Queue

When the time came to leave for college, I got cold feet. I'd finished my sophomore year in town and planned to complete my studies at Harcourt University in Michigan. I had been fine when there was an ocean between my folks and me, but suddenly a two-day ride from Chicago to Michigan seemed so far. I'd been trying to back out of it for days.

Dad was in the garage, piling my belongings into the Buick. "Who am I, Superman? Give me a hand, Joan. Forget the hi-fi, I can't fit it in."

"Maybe I shouldn't go away to school. I could finish up right here." I was ashamed of being scared. It didn't make sense that I, a cosmopolitan European traveler, was afraid of living on a college campus.

"We already paid a year's tuition. You're going!" insisted my mother from the kitchen. The woman had ears like radar.

You've just got stage fright. Once you get settled, you'll be the star of the show." Dad always looked on the sunny side.

Miriam came outside, frowning. "Stop exaggerating. She'll adjust like everyone else."

***

Bronze leaves crackled beneath our feet as we dragged my suitcases to Butler Hall Girls' Dormitory. My stomach hurt. When we finally found my dorm room, my new roommate and her parents looked up from their unpacking.

"Hi, I'm Margaret," said a bookish girl.

"And hello to you, Margaret!" Irv flashed his best toothy smile.

"Well, I guess you girls won't worry about your weight with this walk everyday," groaned Miriam, as she fell into the nearest chair.

I turned to cast a warning look in her direction and noticed something strange. As my dad extended his hand to Margaret's father, I thought I saw a hesitation.

"We're Irving and Miriam Lazlow, and this is our daughter Joan."

Her parents stiffened. There was no mistaking it. "I'm Bradley Johnsen, this is my wife Henrietta, and you've met my daughter, Margaret." Margaret's smile seemed sincere. What was going on?

A couple of days later, I found out.

"My parents are so narrow-minded," Margaret blurted out after a tense phone call. I thought she was going to cry. "After meeting your family, they went directly to the Dean of Women to request a Christian roommate for me."

I tried to stay calm. "I guess they didn't have much luck, huh?"

"That's right. They were turned down, and I'm glad! They can be really stupid sometimes, but please, Joan, I don't want you to take it personally."

How could I not be offended? How did they know my religion at first glance? Had the Nazis come to America?

This was the first time I'd experienced discrimination. Back then, it would make me doubt myself and feel ashamed of who I was. It would be years before I could stand up to people who allow their fear to make them cruel.

***

The Hebrew holy days fell within a week of our new semester. It was traditional for all Jewish students to attend the annual holiday dance. I was really getting lonely and thought I could at least try it. That morning, I sat disconsolate on the library steps looking at all the strange faces in the quad. This would surely be torture.

Maybe I'll catch the first train back to Chicago. I hated the social pressure of a Stag and Drag, where secretly terrified girls and boys feigned nonchalance. In Chicago they had at least been held in swanky hotels with glitzy ballrooms. Here it was in a musty student lounge. Being touched by strange boys in a redecorated basement didn't seem like the wholesome entertainment it was meant to be.

I arrived late and eased my way down a steep staircase into a roomful of Chinese lanterns spattered with Stars of David dangling in semi-darkness. This dimly lit business frightened me. *This place is spooky, and it smells dank.* I snatched the last steel bridge chair, my fortress for the evening.

A pimply face approached me, "Would you like to dance?" it cracked.

"Thanks, but I'll sit this one out. I don't like rock 'n' roll."

My mouth was dry but since I'd staked out a safety zone, it seemed wiser to die of thirst than to vacate my chair. A pair of horn-rimmed glasses approached—

"I'm Bob Klein, wanna dance?"

"Thanks, Bob, but I have a very bad headache." Again, I saw the slumped shoulders and quick retreat. I felt guilty rejecting these guys. I knew it took guts to ask someone to dance.

This was too painful. I had to get out of it. As I grabbed my coat and darted toward freedom, a handsome, older guy swerved in front of me, obstructing the door.

"Hi! I'm Dave Goldman and I've been watching you, trying to think of some clever line."

I looked up into confident, deep-blue eyes. He looked amused and determined all at once, and carried his tweed suit with casual elegance. He wasn't a boy; he was a man.

The words came to me more slowly than with the others, "I…I'm sorry, I was just leaving."

"Yeah, this is a boring party. But maybe I could walk you to the dorm?"

"I'm a law student. Third year. From Boston. How about you? New girl I'll bet."

"You're right. Fresh from Chicago. I must look pretty lost."

"You just look pretty." He smiled and suddenly looked shy, like a little boy. Conversation with him was easy. I found myself babbling on about Anne Frank and my adventures in Europe

Dave Goldman must have known I was a newcomer because I'd never heard of him or his big-man-on-campus reputation. My gossipy schoolmates soon clued me in.

"Well, Joan, how did you snare our darling Dave of the airwaves?" a rotund redhead cooed after he'd left.

"What are you talking about?"

"Dave's radio show is a campus hit. He's got the sexiest voice ever," the redhead's friend chimed in.

They looked at me expectantly.

"Yes, he is quite a charmer," I finally replied. I knew they expected to hear one of those "across a crowded room" stories, but I just didn't have one.

A few days later, Dave managed to talk me into going together to Day of Atonement services at temple. By 8:30 AM, a crowd of students and some locals had gathered before the doors of the men's gymnasium, now a makeshift synagogue. They'd transformed the room with large baskets of flowers and a podium for the rabbi. An ark of the covenant, a large walnut cabinet, housed the holy scrolls of the Old Testament.

"They did a good job on it," I commented to Dave.

"Yeah, but those basketball hoops are a real eyesore." He pulled a white skullcap and prayer shawl from a little black-velvet pouch he'd been holding. Most of the men wore skullcaps, but few carried their personal prayer shawls. Dave stood up and with a robust flourish, swept it around his shoulders. He seemed gratified by its effect on me. He smiled, "My family is descended from ancient priests."

Students checked each other out through the entire service, male and female necks bobbing and weaving in every direction. Religious cruising. I scanned the crowded room, too.

Suddenly my eyes fell upon a face right across the aisle. It was heart-shaped without a trace of paint. I'd seen lips like those in museum portraits, never in real life. I was transfixed.

It was like I'd known her before—the arch of the eyebrows, the shape of her nose, the luminous long black hair. We made brief eye contact, and my toes tingled. I turned away quickly. A few seconds later, I stole a second glance in her direction to get a better look but flushed red when I realized she'd never taken her eyes from me.

I felt faint. Our eyes locked again. She was looking at me in a way no girl had before. She wasn't assessing my clothes or makeup—she was taking me in, shameless in her gaze. I panicked and wanted to escape. I prayed for the rabbi to sense my urgency and end the service. *Oh, what's the big deal? I can appreciate her good looks the way one appreciates a sculpture or a painting. There's nothing wrong with that.*

Still, when the rabbi finally blessed us and the ceremony ended, I planned a hasty retreat. *I'll lean on David.* "Would you mind if we leave through the side door? I'm not feeling well." *She'll see we're an item, and I'm not some kind of weirdo.*

The next morning,, an insistent knock startled me out of a deep sleep. I flung open the door.

"Hi, I'm Cindy. My roommate Joyce and I live across the hall. Our phone's on the fritz. May I use yours?" Exaggerated innocence widened her incredible sapphire eyes. I went numb.

"Sure, go ahead. I'm Joan Lazlow, nice to meet you"

While she waited on the line, she turned toward me, "You were at services yesterday. You wore a blue dress, right?"

"Yes, that's right. And you wore green," I pronounced, with the objectivity of Marie Curie examining the effects of radiation. I was trying to be cool, nothing could have been less consequential than that dress.

"Was that your boyfriend?"

"Not exactly. He's a new friend," I answered, feeling uncomfortable. She hung up the phone.

"But you're hoping he'll be your boyfriend, right? For a new friend, he seemed to act like he owned you."

"Are you looking to snare my almost-boyfriend?" I affected a mock schoolteacher pose, and she laughed the prettiest laugh I'd ever heard. We became friends right on the spot. In the next few days, this easy banter would become our style. I felt a kinship to her so immediate and real that Michigan didn't seem so bad anymore. Later that week, Cindy walked me to the campus beauty shop.

"So what are you having done, Joanie?"

"I need a perm, this mop is driving me crazy."

"Really? I thought you were a natural," she winked knowingly. Scared and excited, I wondered just how much she knew.

"I bet you're trying to copy that brunette's hairdo from the library yesterday. Don't think I didn't watch you ogle her."

"I wasn't ogling, she reminded me of someone back in high school." *Was she jealous?*

"When you're done let's go shopping."

"No, I can't," I replied, knowing she would talk me into it. "Cindy, it's not a good idea."

"Come on, don't be a drip." She kept pushing, as usual. "There's a new Saks Fifth Avenue downtown, and afterwards we'll get a cherry coke."

"This is the last time"

"Sure.

"Really."

"Of course."

It wouldn't be the last time. It never was. But being with her was worth the risk. I hated separating from Cindy to attend classes. Even worse was sharing her company with the other girls in the dining hall. That problem was temporarily solved when our dorm boycotted the lousy food. We started eating together at a drugstore coffee shop every evening.

One night Dad phoned, agitated, "Joan, are you ill?"

"No, Dad, why?"

I heard Miriam shouting in the background, "If she's not sick, then she's a drug addict!"

"Why the $300 drug bill last month?"

"I've been eating at Joe's Drugstore. The dorm is on strike; the food in the dining hall is poison."

"I'm paying a fortune for the food over there, and you're on strike!" he snarled. "Kids today are all prima donnas— during the Depression, we weren't so fussy. We were lucky to have a crust of bread!"

"Dad, times have changed!"

Joe's coffee shop smelled of rubbing alcohol and grease. The food area was separated from the pharmacy by a wooden trellis covered in phony red and white roses, but it was heaven to me.

* * *

"I bet English is a snap, but your chemistry classes must be tough," I made small talk, warming up to my treasured evening meal with Cindy. The waiter's interruption was an unbearable intrusion on these rare moments alone. "Yes, yes," I brushed him off, "we'll have hamburgers and shakes. Is that okay with you, Cindy?"

"Sure Joanie," she rested her elbow on the table, "I love someone to order for me, it's very sexy." *I shouldn't have done that, this isn't a date! She probably flirts with guys the way she's flirting with me now. If only I could touch that olive skin.*

After a few polite questions about my classes, there was a lull in conversation. Cindy leaned toward me, "Joanie, you have the most gorgeous bedroom eyes."

I stopped breathing. The room spun. This must be the feeling other girls describe about boys. With my insides churning, I could only stare at my plate, my face and neck red hot.

"Doesn't your new boyfriend tell you how pretty you are?"

"Sometimes, maybe." I avoided her eyes. *How can she say such things?*

As we walked back to the dorm in the twilight, I wondered if anyone noticed our shoulders nearly touching. I flushed at the thought. That night, I lay awake, struggling with what had just happened. *I can't be in orbit over a girl.* Kenny Mason's face floated before my eyes, still haunting me. "Why are you in love with a dead girl?" *I can't be stuck on girls, dead or alive girls. It's wrong. I'm out of my mind. I'll make myself snap out of this stupidity.*

Despite the innocent façade of the '50s, the pressure to fit in could be menacing. Of course I wanted to be accepted, and in campus life it was apparent that a girl's passport to popularity was the man in her life. So as any other college co-ed, aspiring to the impossible ideal of perfect clothes, perfect hair and the perfect companion, I reserved weekends for my steady boyfriend Dave. Meanwhile, Cindy became foremost contender for the pin of ZBT president Don Peters.

On Wednesday afternoons, Dave used his radio show as a forum to declare his unending devotion to "my little angel, Joanie, in Butler Hall."

"Joan, come here quickly!" yelled a girl in the dorm, *Chances Are* wafting from her room. "Dave's playing your song! Couldn't you just die? He's the most romantic guy. You're so lucky. She dragged me into her room and turned it up, lest I miss one pearl flowing from Dave's golden throat. I pulled away, annoyed. His attentions made me uncomfortable, and my lack of interest was disturbing. I preferred to live sealed off in my private life with Cindy.

ZBT Don drove the "make-out car," a sharp blue Olds convertible that hosted our double dates practically every Saturday night. Cindy and Don sat in front, and Dave and I sat in back. I hated watching Cindy cuddle up to him, but I felt obligated to do the same with Dave. I didn't understand anything about my feelings for Cindy. One moment I longed to kiss her on the mouth and in the next, felt appalled by the ugly, terrible thought!

I doubly resented Dave for taking the place of Cindy and

thought he was being a little greedy with me. After all, he had our daily phone conversations and a lingering Saturday night kiss in the dorm lobby. Lately he was pushing for study time together. It was all too much, and I turned him down with any excuse I could find.

It crushed me when Cindy began flirting with Dave. She would answer my phone and talk to him while I worked on assignments. Meanwhile, it sent me through the roof. *Why is she throwing herself at him?* It wasn't Cindy talking suggestively to Dave that hurt, rather it was her ignoring me. I felt discarded.

One afternoon, as she giggled her way through a particularly long conversation with him, I fumed at my desk. When she hung up, I slammed my book shut, a fire welling up from my chest into my face.

"Are you in love with Dave?" I demanded. "Tell me now, Cindy! Tell me the truth. Your flirting is making me sick!"

Cindy's jaw dropped. "Flirting? Dave's cute, but he's hardly my type," she stared languidly at the bulletin board near my closet, filled with photos of the four of us. "I want a husband with gobs of money." She plopped on the bed across from my desk, her sapphire eyes clouded with surprise. "I'm your friend, Joanie. I wouldn't steal your guy. Besides, Dave is nuts about you."

"Oh, Cindy, he thinks you're beautiful."

"*You* think I'm beautiful."

I flushed. Cindy rolled onto her back and turned her head to the side, staring at her reflection in the mirror across the room. "Listen, dummy, you hand me the phone everyday. I talk to him because you'll lose him if I don't." She sat up abruptly. "I gotta study. This whole thing is stupid. Wake up, you're pushing him away!"

"Maybe that's true." I curled up in a ball on the bed next to her. I didn't want her to leave.

"Think about it," she scowled, "You give me the phone, then accuse me of trying to steal him! You're nuts!"

"Yeah, I guess you're right." I couldn't tell her what really hurt me. Her attention was being stolen from me. She laughed her most adorable laugh, "It's okay, Joanie, the next time he calls, talk to him no matter what. Deal?"

"Deal," I mumbled, as Cindy brushed past Margaret on her way out. "Hey, Margaret, how's the biology coming along?"

"I'm not a whiz kid like you."

"I'd be willing to help you anytime…" Cindy tossed her hair and winked, grinning wickedly at her.

Margaret never even looked up, "Sure, thanks, that's nice of you."

***

Dave called several times that afternoon.

"Are you ignoring me? I'm tired of Cindy fielding my calls."

Maybe Cindy was right. Dave hadn't enjoyed the phone chats. This made no sense at all. How could he not love Philadelphia High School's most popular girl?

"Let's meet at the library right now. I promise not to distract you—although most girls find me very distracting," he chuckled.

I didn't want to leave, in case Cindy came back. "No, I'm studying in the dorm."

"Do what you want!" His voice was icy. As the line went dead, I felt frightened, then relieved.

I didn't hear from him for two days. On the third, he stood waiting at the bottom of the stairs after my last class. He grabbed my bag as always, put his other arm around my waist, and walked me back to Butler Hall. It was as if my indifference intrigued him instead of pushing him away. He was determined to have what he wanted. Maybe I was lucky to have someone who refused to let me push him away.

That October, Dave and I strolled a wooded path and sat down on a bench near a lily pond.

"Little bundle of contradictions, can you tell me exactly what it is? What does contradiction mean?"

"That's from Anne Frank! Dave, you memorized it!" I threw my arms around his neck, so grateful to him for his tenderness and caring.

He felt something real for me…and it broke my heart. *Oh God, I'm not in love with him. Why can't I be in love? Why?*

"Hey, if this is what it takes, I'll memorize the whole darn book—backwards! You make me crazy, Joanie. Sometimes, like today, you can be so warm and loving. Other times, you look right past me. I can't ever predict which way you'll be."

This is it. Soon he'll realize something is so awfully wrong with me. Having to lie, even to myself, hurt so many people. The safest way out was to keep my secret.

***

"Don't you absolutely adore this dress?" Cindy twirled before the floor-length mirror in my room, modeling her strapless aqua chiffon ball gown.

"You're beautiful, Cindy. Don will go ape when he sees you falling out of that number." *I hate Don so much I could blast his pasty ZBT face right off the face of the earth.*

"Maybe it's too revealing. Maybe you don't approve," Cindy teased, "after all, you only wear classic, conservative gowns. Not that they aren't exquisite."

"Well, that dress is a knockout," I gulped.

"Help unzip me, I'm trapped." She twirled again, taking a last admiring look in the mirror. Her sight and smell made me dizzy.

I hated encouraging her, resenting the display for those guys. *We could just dump them. We'll go through life as a team: Cindy the prize-winning chemist and Joan her devoted helper.*

We were friendly to all the dorm girls, but my proprietary attitude toward Cindy and her love of the constant attention made our friendship very exclusive. Everyone got the hint except for Charise Motsky. She lived down the hall and seemed able to detect my scent from behind closed doors. Her chipmunk jowls and tailored slacks gave me the creeps.

She also shot me looks. Weird long looks. The more indifferent I behaved, the harder she clung. One morning, she intercepted me on the way to the shower.

"Joan, would you be interested in bunking with me next semester? Sylvia is moving out, and I have a corner room with lots of windows. You'd love it. Say yes. Pretty please? Say yes right now!"

"Thanks, Charise, but I've already made plans," I barely hid my contempt. She shuffled away dispirited. I was shocked by her audacity. What could she be thinking?

Midterms came and went, and Cindy and I had scored highest in our dorm. The residents of Butler came to the Dean of Women's luncheon to honor us. I writhed from embarrassment at the banquet table. Cindy's roommate Joyce compounded my discomfort by slipping into the chair next to me.

"Cindy is conceited and selfish. You're wasting your time on a real pill," Joyce whispered. "You don't know her like I do, Joan"

"Stop it, I don't want to hear any more!" I balled up my napkin, resisting the urge to stuff it in her mouth.

"You'll be sorry you didn't listen to me. Listen, you're a nice girl. Just look out for her, she's trouble."

At first, I couldn't understand what had gotten into Joyce, but the next Saturday night I began to see what she meant. After the dance, several girls gathered in Cindy and Joyce's room to rehash the evening. The aqua dress had been a big hit, and the crowd sat three deep Indian-style to hear Cindy's exploits.

"Joanie, would you like to see how my kisses drive Don wild?" Her audience snickered.

Joyce shushed everyone. "That's perverted, Cindy, someone will report you."

I hesitated, but decided to play along. We were just kidding, right? Why not play the game? I rose from the bed and walked toward her.

Those Siamese cat eyes never left my face as she took my hand, turned it palm up, and pressed her mouth deep inside.

I felt her moist lips sucking into my flesh and trembled. Had anyone noticed? The room became still. Every cell in my body was responding to the sensation. Surely the girls felt the sexual tension in the air and perhaps felt guilty themselves for knowing it.

A slight smile crossed Cindy's lips. She was well aware of the audience she held rapt and quite proud of what she was doing to me. My eyes fell away, and I eased backward. The girls, unwilling voyeurs, exchanged tense looks.

I laughed. "Well, I'll have to try that on Dave sometime."

That night I slept fitfully, replaying the scene in my head. *How am I going to face those girls tomorrow? What do they think of us?*

I took my usual seat in the cafeteria at breakfast, but the previous night's audience had chosen other tables. Only Joyce and Margaret remained. Cindy nonchalantly slipped into the seat across from me. I searched her eyes.

"Did you notice that Mary, Suzanne, and Arlene are ignoring us?"

"Who cares?" Cindy was aloof.

"Obviously, it's because you two acted like idiots last night," snipped Joyce. "Cindy, I warned you."

Cindy stuck out her tongue, and they giggled. With the tension somewhat broken, Margaret stroked my hand. "Don't worry, it's not important where they sit. Nothing could've been that big a deal, Joanie."

"That's right," Cindy echoed.

My stomach was killing me. Margaret's kind words didn't console me. It had been a very big deal. Unfortunately, I was too wrapped up in Cindy to see how big it would get.

***

That Friday, Margaret's dad phoned. Her grandmother was severely ill, and Margaret had to go to Chicago. I decided to invite Cindy to sleep over and see what the other night had really been about. She'd quickly accepted the invitation to "help me cram for my history exam."

I had been nervous all day. *She said she'd meet me after chemistry lab at about 8. It's already 8:30. She's not coming. I don't care. Yes I do. Oh my God, she's knocking on my door.*

"May I come in? It's Cindy."

"Sure," I said, too quickly.

She wore a pink flannel nightgown. I sat on the edge of my bed in my red-and-white striped pajamas, not knowing what to expect. She leaned seductively against the closed door, and said softly, "How about if we both sleep in your bed tonight?" *How could she be so bold? Can this be happening?*

I fought to catch my breath and moved over against the wall. Cindy slithered next to me. I turned on my back with my hands at my sides, staring awkwardly at the ceiling, feeling the heat of her body, numb with fear and afraid to even move. *What should I do? Should I do anything? If I touch her, she'll probably run screaming down the halls.*

After a few grueling minutes, Cindy propped herself up on one elbow and kissed my ear. "Hi, bedroom eyes," she whispered. And just like that, I knew. I drew her close to me, my body aching as I felt her lips touching mine. I fumbled under her nightgown and began tentatively caressing her breasts. My fingertips tingled as I kneaded her tawny skin.

Neither of us disrobed. I was still afraid of being pushed away and made no attempt to reach below her waist. Instead I eased open her mouth with my palm, and she let me explore every mysterious groove with my tongue. She sighed and then pulled me on top of her. I pushed deeply into her warm groin. She didn't resist, as I feared, but she moaned and dug her nails into my shoulders while her flannel-clad pelvis undulated beneath me. Suddenly her body tightened and shuddered. Was this orgasm? There were tears gathered in the corners of her eyes.

"Cindy! I'm sorry, did I hurt you?"

"No, I'm happy. Don't you know you're a wonderful lover?"

Lover? Everyone knows boys are lovers, not girls!

***

I woke up at sunrise overwhelmed by nausea that sent me running to the bathroom. I hid there feeling so alone, so ashamed. Yet there was no doubt in my mind that I'd been searching the world for someone like Cindy without realizing it. I felt alive and completed, simply by touching the softness of her body. There could be no greater pleasure than feeling her heart beat against mine, no greater joy than merging inside her thighs. I lived to inhale her rain forest scent and touch her. What was so wrong about that? What could be right about it? Surely people didn't feel like this about their own sex.

Still, I went right back to the scene of the crime. Cindy's eagerness made me oblivious to risk. I agreed to meet that night, feeling less frightened, less guilty. This time we discarded the pajamas and nightgown. Our moist interlocked bodies and the flame in my soul eclipsed all reason. This *was* right. How could it not be?

We hadn't slept for two nights. By Sunday morning we were fast asleep when Charise Motsky tapped lightly before throwing open the door. The tapping had barely brought me to consciousness, but the sound of the door made me bolt straight up. Our eyes locked; mine frantic, Charise's triumphant and cruel. I yanked the blanket up over my chest.

Charise had found us sharing one bed. We were doomed. She giggled, mumbling something like "Let's go, homo," and raced back into the hall shutting the door behind her.

"Cindy! Cindy, wake up!" I shook her bare shoulder. Charise Motsky just saw us in bed together!"

"So what, Joanie? That girl's pathetic. What would there be for her to tell?"

3 White Gardenias

I sat on my bed staring at the phone. It had been more than 48 hours since I'd heard Cindy's voice. One weekend—one crazy, wonderful weekend—had given her complete control of my life. *Where is she? What's she doing? Is she thinking about me?*

Tuesday already. I walked around the room and stared at Margaret's carefully made bed. Why hadn't she returned? *Did her grandmother die?* I ran my fingertips along the frosty windowpane. September was a miserable month. The clouds were a heavy gray, and soon everything would be buried in snow. Everything—buried.

I can't stand it! I'll call her. My hand shook, and my stomach cramped up tighter with every ring. No answer...

I never should have touched her.

Joan, you were brought up well. Now look at you. What would your father say? Dad would probably make a joke.

Maybe nothing really happened. But no, I can still feel Cindy on my skin, lying on top of her and reaching out to her breasts, running my fingers through her hair, the scent of rain forest everywhere...Enough!

I push books around the shelf, feverishly searching for my medieval history text. *It's no use. The bookplates all resemble Cindy.*

The pages fall open at Eleanor of Aquitane. *Eleanor was banished when she displeased King Henry. Maybe I'll be banished for immoral conduct and have to hide away—like Anne Frank.* Stop! I force my thoughts back to my schoolwork, determined not to let her rule every moment of my life.

At noon, I stepped out of the elevator and peered through the glass doors into the dining hall, trying to spot Cindy. I wouldn't sit with her; she hated me. Where could I go? Charise Motsky was already inside, stuffing her face. She'd probably told her weird pals that she saw us in bed together.

I avoided their table and darted to the food bank. Grabbing a tray and snatching a hot dog from the steamer, I searched for a friendly face. Joyce waved me over to join her table. *Oh, Lord, no. Cindy's there!* My throat felt dry, and my knees felt wobbly. *Should I sit there? Should I sit alone? If she ignores me, I'll kill myself for sure. What if she thinks I followed her?*

"Hi, Joyce, how was your weekend?"

Cindy didn't look up. She remained engrossed in conversation with Phyllis Carson, her lab partner. *No long looks. No rapt attention. Now she's cold and removed. She snared her prey and moved on, the little vixen. I hate that little snot. And I want her more than ever!*

"Oh no, look at the time, I'm late for physics!" Cindy jumped up from the table. "Bye girls, see you later." There was nothing in her face for me. It was as if nothing had ever happened. If Charise did talk about us, it certainly wasn't revealed in Cindy's expression, though she kept her distance from me. I thought about suicide, but didn't have the guts.

At least I'd see her Saturday night at the much anticipated Winter Swoon. Surely she'd speak to me there. She'd never make a scene by snubbing me at the dance, not in front of Don.

Saturday night, I sat in the lobby of Butler Hall amazed that this was the same boring lobby I passed through every day. It was pulsating with excited girls, making last-minute adjustments to their nylons and heels, creating a hum like a swarm of bees. I peeked over my shoulder into a mirror. *God forbid my nylons should be askew.*

Dave was the first guy to arrive. He adorned my burgundy gown with a fragrant corsage of white gardenias. He bent and kissed me lightly on the cheek.

"You leave me speechless, Joanie, so elegant."

No doubt about it, he was handsome in his black shark-skin suit. When I attached a white carnation to his lapel, he beamed, "Joanie, I'm the proudest guy in the world."

Heads swiveled from our left and right as we passed through the doors of the dance. The vast gymnasium glistened with a festoon of lights. An orchestra struck up the school anthem, building excitement. Then a drum roll signaled Dave's triumphant moment, his call to come forward to receive that year's Outstanding Service Award.

Everyone was clapping and whistling. Dave gave them a gallant military salute. Then he pointed into the crowd. It took a moment for me to realize that he was motioning for me to come up to the stage to join him. The shock wiped the phony demure smile right off my face. I recovered a tight grin as I mounted the steps to the dais. *Oh God, what if they knew, what if he knew, what a fraud I am? "Don't you be a fool," my mother's voice admonished. "He's smart and good-looking, and he'll be a good provider."*

The conductor struck up the first notes of *Chances Are*. Dave whisked me onto the dance floor, and into the safety of other swaying dancers. Cindy whirled by, wrapped in Dan's arms. The plunging folds of her aqua chiffon gown revealed more than a suggestion of those velvety breasts. Hadn't I tasted them just a few nights before? I knew her body, yet I wasn't permitted to display affection, ask her to dance or look into her eyes. A week ago she had been mine. And now?

Cindy and Don approached. Don shook Dave's hand and winked at me. "You must be proud of your guy, Joan"

I cringed as that phony smile again took over my face. Cindy silently patted Dave on the shoulder. She looked through me. *I could slap that gorgeous face!*

As they folded into the crowd, I remarked to Dave, "Cindy's dress is beautiful, don't you think?" Dave held me tighter as we moved to the Tennessee Waltz, and I caught a glimpse of Cindy's drop-dead dimples flashing at Don. *She's probably playing us both for fools.*

"Joanie, she can't compare to you in looks." Dave kissed my cheek. "Did you notice Cindy was a bit cold toward you? Come on, give me the gossip," he smiled, "have you girls had a spat?"

"No, we're fine. She just gets moody sometimes." *It's only half a lie.*

"Yeah, Don tells me she's quite a project."

I wanted to ask what else he'd said, but I dropped the subject. I soon lost sight of Cindy. All hope of speaking to her evaporated when she disappeared from the room with Don.

That night at the dorm I stood in the hallway contemplating knocking on Cindy's door. No good, it would wake her roommate. I though about phoning her from my room. I had to find out why she'd ignored me. Was she scared that Charise Motsky had told everyone she'd seen us together in one bed?

I gave up on the idea of calling from my room. My roommate was probably there studying, so I couldn't speak freely anyway. Margaret's religion forbade dancing. *I wish I could tell Margaret about my torment, but she wouldn't understand. No one could understand.* Any normal person would disapprove. I disapproved! If our secret got out, my parents would disown me, and Cindy's would ship her back to Philadelphia.

Well, great! I didn't want to be a weirdo anyway. I'll show her—I'll forget her, too.

Monday night, Cindy found me alone in the laundry room. My muscles tightened when I saw her, carrying her bag of dirty clothes. She smiled as she brushed past. The acrid smell of bleach scratched at the tissues inside my nostrils as I slouched on a bench staring at the dryers. Maybe my stare would make them explode.

Cindy spoke in a casual tone while pumping dimes into a dryer.

"Hey, Joanie, would you like to get a room with me off campus next fall?"

I froze. The anguish of feeling invisible to her the past days and nights welled into fury.

"Have I missed something here? You'd like to live with me, but you don't want to talk to me?" I avoided her eyes and poured pink detergent into the washer. The pastel powder reminded me of her flannel pajamas.

"I had to be by myself." Cindy's voice trembled. "I had a lot of thinking to do. That's how I sort things out."

"So because you had thinking to do, I could get lost? I don't appreciate the way you sort things out, Cindy. You just sort your friends out of your life!" I was growling at her so fiercely I barely recognized myself.

"That's the problem, Joanie, we aren't just friends. Get off your high horse and listen!" Her voice was shrill and urgent. "We need an off-campus apartment"

"Wouldn't that be too expensive?" I could imagine my parents' reaction to such an idea.

"No, not much more than the dorm."

She was just getting warmed up. "We could get jobs when we go home for summer break, and only our meals would be extra. And, Joanie, we'd have more privacy."

Confused, I started to babble nonsense, "Gosh, Cindy, I'd been hoping we could be roommates next semester, right here in Butler"

Cindy stiffened, kicked the dryer and spat at me, "Hard work doesn't appeal to you, right little princess? Forget it." She stalked out.

My head pounded. I was thrilled to death and more scared than I'd ever been. Why hadn't I jumped at the chance to live with her?

***

The following afternoon I poured over my philosophy assignment in the oak-paneled student lounge, when I heard the tinkle of Cindy's voice greeting friends at the door. I glanced over at some girls gathered around a table in the center of the room, studying maps. My face flushed at the sight of her, and I checked to see if they noticed. *She's right, we've got to get out of here.* She smiled that dimpled smile and sat next to me on the Victorian corner sofa.

"Hi," she whispered softly, "Did you ask your parents?"

"Ask what?"

"If you can live off campus, dummy!"

"Sure, it's fine with them," I lied. "My dad will give me back my old secretarial job for the summer." *I'll have to think of a good reason for leaving the dorm.*

She beamed. "Fabulous! Tomorrow we'll get the paper and start looking for rooms."

One of the map-readers, a friend of Cindy's, looked our way. Was she eavesdropping? I stopped breathing. Trying to look nonchalant, I asked, "What about your folks?"

Her face hardened, "They don't care where I live as long as I pull straight A's. My dad graduated magna cum laude from Harcourt, and he expects the same from me. One B and I'm sunk. They'd pull me out of school."

I bumped her shoulder playfully, "They would never do that. Your parents love you. They want the best for you"

She recoiled. "You don't get it, Joanie. I don't have a father who phones me every Sunday or a mother who sends me care packages with imported sardines"

"But I'm sure they love you," I insisted, "...you're wonderful!"

"I don't want to talk about this anymore." A shadow crossed her face, warning me to clam up.

I had so many questions. How could someone so young be experienced at lovemaking? Had there been girls before me? What about boys? Was she easy? I was afraid to pry into her life; she might get offended and never speak to me again. I hated feeling dependent on her every mood, but I was scared to lose her. And scared to be found out by the dorm girls, my parents and the world.

***

Several days later Cindy's roommate Joyce received a

message summoning her home for the weekend. At breakfast in the dining hall, Charise Motsky delivered the note. She shot me a filthy leer. I looked across the table into Cindy's eyes. They practically glistened.

When Cindy and I were alone in the elevator, I suggested a scheme. "On Friday afternoons they serve those awful huevos rancheros in the dining hall. We'll both order them and then say we have stomach cramps. Maybe get some medicine from the nurse. 'Help! We have food poisoning. Call an ambulance!'" Cindy enjoyed the idea.

"We won't make that big a deal," I cautioned, "just act sick enough to cancel our plans with the guys."

"Joanie, where did you learn to be such a good liar?"

I wondered the same thing. What we were doing was destroying everything I believed in, all that I knew to be right and good. Anne Frank, Otto and Miep would be ashamed of me. I hated myself for lying. But Lord knows, all I could think about was Cindy's touch.

The boys never questioned our sincerity. They figured if we were missing our dates with them, we must be sick.

***

Friday night Cindy and I shared a pizza and beer at a campus hangout. The fake red-leather booths were small, and wine-stained oilcloths covered the craggy wooden tables. Faded travel posters of Italy adorned the rough cement walls. Used Chianti bottles, splattered with wax, served as candleholders. It was early, and we were the sole patrons. For me, this crummy joint was the most romantic place in the world.

Cindy's eyes grew deeper blue in the candle's glow. She pinched my thigh under the table. "What are you getting, the anchovy pizza?"

"Maybe I should; then I wouldn't have to offer you a bite." I crossed my legs, deliberately bumping hers.

I had no appetite for food. We talked. We flirted. We rushed home.

I crept into her room and slid between the perfumed

sheets. Her naked skin startled me.

"I'll keep you warm little girl," she muttered. Caressing my face with one hand, she unbuttoned my pajama top and unsnapped the bottoms. Tiny kisses delighted my eyelids as she rolled onto me. She flicked and teased my lips before plunging her soft tongue deep into my mouth. I sucked in its deliciousness. I felt teeth nipping my throat and hands kneading my breasts, while a ravenous tongue journeyed over my body, at last coming to rest between my legs. Her tongue slowly entered then withdrew, raising me to a fever pitch as I tensed and relaxed with each delirious wave of pleasure. Suddenly I gasped and cried out. She clasped my mouth shut with her palm.

"We can't be overheard! Not here, not now."

She pressed her pelvis firmly against my aching mound in an unrelenting, undulating motion that brought me to tears. I'd become one with her. There could be no greater happiness. As I struggled to sit up, she eased my head back against the lilac-scented pillow.

"We've just begun"

Cindy turned me onto my stomach. I felt exposed. *What is she doing?* She was in total control, running her delicate hands along my backside. I felt her soft lips traveling down my spine, her tongue filling hidden crevices. Her fingers reached deep inside me—tender, forceful, insistent. She filled me. I exploded into a thousand particles of joy. "Joanie," she whispered, "you're a virgin everywhere and you're mine. I love your eyes and her lips." We rested, listening to each other breathe. We didn't speak.

Finally I blurted out, "You don't go all the way with Don, do you?" She smiled that enigmatic smile and snuggled into my breasts.

I longed to ask if she were in love with me. Maybe this was just play, but it felt like love to me. *Everyone knows serious love is always between men and women, not girls.* I kept silent. I couldn't bear it if she pulled away. I'd rather die than never see her again. *How could this be happening to me? I'm proba-bly the only weirdo on campus. Probably the only weirdo in Michigan and all of Illinois. Am I a freak of nature?*

Hoping that the college library would hold the answer, one evening I disguised myself in sun glasses and a ski cap, crept into the reference section, and looked up "lesbian" in an abnormal psychology text. "A female who exhibits unnatural erotic attraction toward another female." Unnatural. I remembered that Hitler put homosexuals into the gas chambers along with the Jews. I became aware of the other people in the library. Could they see what I was reading? I slammed the book shut.

I refuse to be unnatural. I'll accept Dave's invitation Saturday night at his apartment. After dinner I'll go all the way. I know he'll try. I can forget Cindy and be normal again. I went straight to the bookstore and bought a van Gogh poster for Dave. He'd told me van Gogh's "Sunflowers" would be his first million-dollar purchase.

I'd always enjoyed Dave's beatnik apartment he shared with a roommate, Bob. I was elated to be greeted that night by the aroma of sizzling steaks instead of the foul kitchen smells of Butler Hall. The tiny living room glowed from table candles while the Kingston Trio lamented the plight of poor Tom Dooley on the portable record player.

An array of vertical gray bricks shelved the boys' stacks of books and records. Orange crates were end tables. Joan Baez and Woody Guthrie posters hung above the aged sofa. Bob's beat-up guitar lay in a corner near the kitchen. He really wanted to be a folk singer, not an attorney.

I was surprised to see Bob dressed up that night, with perfect Brylcreem comb marks through his dark hair.

"You look sharp, Bob, where are you going?" I asked.

He blushed and smiled, "I'm seeing Roger Williams play downtown with Stephanie." He buffed his left shoe on the back of his right trouser leg. "I'd love to stay and chat, but I'm late. Let's all chew the fat later."

"Hey," Dave called after him, "don't come home too early."

Dave had converted an old card table into an elegant dinette with a white linen cloth. He'd placed an arrangement of white gardenias in the center.

"Well, Joanie, what's in that tube you hid behind the sofa?"

"Here, monsieur." With a slight curtsy, I handed him the tube. He unrolled the poster.

Dave's hug swept me right off the ground. "This is really neat. You're my angel. Let's put it up right now!" He disappeared into the bedroom and returned with a black frame, which miraculously fit the poster. He had it up on the wall in seconds.

"Wow," I said in awe, "you make everything look so effortless. You're a chef, a showman, an artist, a scholar…" If I could have waved a magic wand to be able to love Dave, I would have done it right that minute.

Dave took my hand and sat beside me on the sofa. He cupped my face and said, "Honey, everyone thinks I'm a hot shot, but I know I struggle to pull a B. I'm not a genius, and I'm scared I'll be a lousy lawyer. Maybe I should go into politics."

His honesty warmed me. Maybe I could love him. "That's a great idea! You care about people, and you're a great talker. I think you could be a senator or even president!"

"Joanie, you inspire me. I'll be president and you'll be my first lady."

Was that a proposal? He pulled out my chair and brought out steaks and potatoes on a platter piled high with crunchy onion rings.

"Don't start yet. I have to finish the salad." He came back, bowl in hand. "Do we need anything else?" he flashed his knock-'em-dead grin.

"We just need you to sit down and enjoy it with me." The conversation stopped while we devoured the meal. Just when

I thought I couldn't take another bite, Dave said, "Save room for apple pie."

"Maybe later. I'm stuffed," I clasped my stomach. "You're a sensational chef."

"I'd be glad to cook for you every night," he winked, removing the steak platter.

I grabbed it from his hands. "No you don't. I'll take care of that."

I cleared the table and washed the dishes. *Playing his wife might not be so bad after all.*

Dave put on Jackie Gleason's latest *Music for Lovers Only*, and we twirled around the room pretending to be Fred Astaire and Ginger Rogers. The tempo changed, and he swayed me gently to the sensuous moan of the trombone. He pressed me tightly against him, and I felt a hard bulge in his pants. What was that? *Oh God.* I eased out of his arms.

"Are the prom pictures back yet, Dave?"

"You sure have lousy timing!" He kicked the sofa leg. *Dave's ready for the real thing. What's wrong with me? That's what I'm here for.* We resorted to an hour's necking session on the sofa, during which I obsessively counted the minutes for the buzzer to announce Bob's return.

Relieved I greeted him, "Hi, Bobby, we missed you! How about a Coke?"

"Have a good time with Stephanie?" Dave asked brusquely, annoyed at the intrusion.

"It was all right, but she's a little too pushy for me. Hey, Joan, when are you going to fix me up with your roommate?"

"I'll ask her, but she promised her parents she wouldn't date. They're very religious people."

"Tell her I'm very religious, too," Bob chuckled. We gossiped until midnight. Finally, Dave walked me back to the dorm. We shared a last lingering kiss in the lobby. *A sweet kiss, but why doesn't it stir my soul?*

***

When I got to the room I was happy to see Margaret there, hunched over her microscope.

"Make any discoveries, Louise Pasteur?"

"Nope, nothing new. How was Dave?"

"Just fine, Margaret, I wish you'd go out with Dave's roommate, Bob. He's a swell guy and he says he likes you a lot. God won't punish you." She looked up and laughed.

"I'll date once I'm of legal age. Just wait and see. Keep Bob on ice for me."

Margaret, I couldn't go all the way tonight. And it had nothing to do with good morals. I'm scared I'm abnormal. I wish I had the guts to talk to you.

We changed into our pajamas and turned out the lights. I lay staring into the darkness, alone with Margaret's snores and my fear.

For the next few days, I tried to focus on anything or anyone but Cindy. Nothing helped. On the one hand, I longed to live with her off campus; on the other hand, I was terrified of being found out.

That night when I was washing up in the dorm bathroom, I saw Cindy come in with her toiletries. Using the sink next to mine, she commented, "Guess what! I got a call from the dean's office to set up an appointment for next week. Isn't that neat?"

"I got a call, too," I patted my face dry. "Bet she's going to tell us we're getting scholarships. I heard they give them to all the girls who win the White Orchid Awards. Won't our parents be proud!"

A wistful smile crossed Cindy's lips.

4 The Inquisition

argaret helped me choose a conservative shirt waist dress for my meeting with Dean Potts. A careless appearance could make someone like Mrs. Potts think twice about a scholarship, even if I had proven myself with good grades.

"How do I look?" I gave my hair a disapproving glance.

"Sharp. You look totally sharp, Joanie. The old windbag will hand you the scholarship check right on the spot." Margaret smiled, scooping her slides and microscope into a black case.

***

Dean Potts, a pinched, graying woman, tapped her desk nervously with a fountain pen. Cigarette smoke hung around the room like a menacing mist. A large ceramic ashtray overflowed with the residue of her day.

She offered me a chair opposite her desk. She waited while I sat down, folded her hands primly and leaned slightly forward.

"Charise Motsky left school last week," she said.

I looked at her uncomprehending.

When she spoke again, her eyes seemed as if she were looking at the wall behind me. "Charise signed a complaint against you and Cindy Kramer, charging lesbian behavior on the second floor of Butler Hall."

"It's not true! It's a lie!" My brain was racing in all directions like a crazy flea circus. A million explanations ran through my mind. I tried to force them out of my mouth.

Dean Potts hand shot up. "This is not a discussion, Joan."

Her eyes finally focused on me. Her neck pulled back as if I smelled bad. "This is a very serious charge. Charise maintains that you and Cindy Kramer spent a weekend sharing the same bed. The complaint asserts that Charise's moral sensibilities were so offended that she was forced to withdraw from the university."

"But Dean Potts..."

"You will have a chance to tell your story at the hearing before your dorm mother, Miss Blake, and myself."

"Is that like a trial?" I felt nauseous. I took deep breaths, trying not to be sick all over myself.

"Yes, a trial of sorts," she shifted in her chair. "After a review of the evidence, we will decide whether expulsion for moral turpitude is in order. This, of course, would terminate your pursuit of higher education. Your school transcript will be stamped, 'Not in Good Standing,' and the reason clearly explained. Homosexual behavior is a criminal offense in Michigan."

I've seen movies about trials. Trials get in the paper. It's a criminal offense; I'll probably go to jail. My folks and everybody in Chicago will know I'm a convict. Dazed, I mumbled a question, "When's the hearing?"

"Probably next month." She began shuffling through a stack of papers. "The final decision will be made in early May. That will be all, Joan. You may go."

Somehow I raised myself to a standing position. My knees started to buckle as I staggered from her office. I believed what I'd done with Cindy was immoral, but now I'd learned it was against the law. It was a crime, like theft and murder. I'd performed criminal acts. I was a criminal.

I could hardly breathe. *Get a grip! Calm down! You still have to make it until May.* How could I study for finals? Why should I study for finals, when I'd probably be expelled? Expelled and disowned.

I stared into the ice-caked branches of the trees lining the paths around the campus. I was more frozen than those trees.

Any minute, we'd be the front-page headlines of the *Chicago Tribune*. The papers would carry photos of Cindy and me leaving the hearing. Reporters would swarm the campus. My friends back home would know everything.

***

Margaret returned from class that evening and saw my bleak expression.

"No scholarship, Joan?"

I nodded. I was too ashamed to say anything.

"Seems like they keep moths in their wallets here at Harcourt, doesn't it?" She changed the subject and chattered on. Overwhelmed by gratitude for her sensitivity, I wanted to tell her everything. But if she learned what I'd done, she'd surely double over and vomit.

Later that night, Margaret came into the room, her face ashen. "Joan, we need to talk." She shut the door and sat on my bed.

"I just received a disturbing phone call. I don't know exactly how to say this, but the Dean of Women asked me to sign a complaint against you and Cindy. Joyce told me she received the same call. Every girl on this floor has been approached to sign a complaint against you."

Oh, my God, they all know the truth. I should kill myself right now.

"While I don't approve of what's going on between you and Cindy, it's your business, not the school's. They're waging an all-out witch hunt, and I know from my time on Student Council that it only takes two signed complaints and you're both expelled. They won't even have to go to the trouble of a hearing."

They could expel us without so much as a trial! I felt my face twitch as Margaret's voice became dim and remote. *Of course they'll find another girl willing to sign our death warrant. They'll find a dozen. Nobody here likes me anymore.*

Margaret was staring at me. "Joan, pull yourself together. This crush is going to ruin your life."

"I wish it were a crush. I love Cindy, and I don't know what to do." Tears of shame flooded my face, seeping down into my mouth.

Margaret put her arm around me and stroked my head. "Joan, promise me you'll make an appointment at the counseling center and get some professional help."

I looked into her eyes and saw her deep concern. She touched my heart. Why hadn't I noticed Margaret was such a wonderful person? *Because you only notice Cindy, that's why.*

***

Days and weeks crawled by. Conversation stopped whenever Cindy and I approached a group of girls in the dorm. Margaret had assured me that no one on our floor had signed the statement against us, but that didn't stop the gossiping. The disgrace of being snubbed drove Cindy and me from the student lounge to a seldom-used basement study room.

"It smells down here! It's like being rats in a dungeon, hiding from everyone." Cindy pinched her nose. "It's not fair!"

I took a deep breath. It was time for a serious talk. "Cindy, what are we going to tell them at the hearing?"

She studied my face, "*Why* would you even ask me such a stupid question?" The venom in her voice startled me. "There's obviously nothing to tell, Joan. Nothing went on. Nothing at all."

"What about living together next semester?" I grasped her arm.

She pulled away. "Wake up! Haven't you noticed our future is on trial? There probably won't be a next semester for us."

I winced. This wasn't going away, like adolescent problems that evaporated with age. This was a situation with consequences that could affect the rest of my life.

***

One evening, someone slipped a note under the door of our basement retreat, "Hi, girls, we're funny too. Want to meet us?"

Cindy wadded up the note and hurled it at me.

"Everybody knows! I want to die."

"But honey…"

"Don't ever speak to me that way again!" Her eyes were sinister and empty in a way I hadn't seen before. "You better remember nothing happened between us, Joan. Nothing."

At 8 the following Monday, I woke to the buzz of my clock radio. *Who cares about medieval history? They'll throw me out of school, good grades or not.* I switched off the alarm and buried my face in the pillow.

Although she affected a poised demeanor to the outside world, Cindy stopped attending classes altogether. One Wednesday afternoon, I caught her writing a letter in the deserted dorm lobby.

"Cindy, why are you sitting here? You have chemistry."

"I'm in no mood to take notes. I couldn't care less about my stupid classes." She looked pale and defeated.

"You have to keep going to class, Cindy. We'll deny every thing. You said so yourself, remember? They have no proof against us."

"Proof! Joan, you're a dreamer. They don't need proof, they have Charise's written statement."

"But they weren't able to get any of the other girls to verify it. And Charise didn't see us do anything. We were just sleeping. It's her word against ours."

"Pipe down, we've got company," she pointed to the mailman. "You're close to graduation. Maybe they won't expel you. But I don't care anymore, so leave me alone."

"Cindy," I moved closer to her desk, "we're in this together. We'll find another school. Maybe in London or Paris. Everything will be all rright, I promise." She gave me a wan smile. I wanted to hug her, but I couldn't do anything.

***

To make matters worse, Dave started asking questions. Cindy related a peculiar conversation she'd recently had with him.

"Cindy," he'd asked out of nowhere, "How close are you and Joan?"

"Close as two people can be," she'd responded. Why was he asking such things? Had he heard gossip from Butler Hall? Would he be a witness for the prosecution? And why would Cindy taunt him that way?

I started to worry about Cindy's testimony. Her moods kept shifting up and down. In the morning, she'd appear confident, almost arrogant, but at night she'd be at the bottom of an emotional pit. She was so young, only a sophomore; she might crack up and blame me for everything.

***

On March 1, we were ushered into the conference room of Butler Hall. Dean Potts sat stiffly at the head of the rectangular table. In her role as dorm mother, Miss Blake sat at the other end, with Brenda, her collie, at her feet.

Miss Blake, a grad student, was blind, and as such insisted her instincts were far superior to those of sighted people. When I denied all the allegations, she'd probably "feel" the lies.

Cindy and I were seated across from each other at the table. Sitting erect with her ankles neatly crossed beneath a starched crinoline slip, she looked like a cover girl for *Seventeen* magazine. The picture of virtue, her flawless complexion attested to innocent femininity. Our pastel shirtwaist dresses and white bobby socks defied any suggestion of Gertrude Stein and Alice B. Toklas.

Dr. Potts, the prosecutor, tapped her pen against the rim of her glass ashtray. "Although this is extremely distasteful, we must proceed now." She reached inside her portfolio, took out a legal-looking paper and read the charges.

"I, Charise Motsky, have witnessed the fact that Joan Lazlow and Cindy Kramer practice lesbianism in Butler Hall. This behavior offends my moral sensibilities and forces me to withdraw from Harcourt University."

Dean Potts left out the part about the two of us sharing one bed. It was probably too disgusting to read out loud.

Dean Potts's cigarette smoke spiraled into a white circular cloud that settled above her head and reminded me of renderings of the devil in my text of Dante's *Inferno*. Potts shot out her first question without a trace of embarrassment. I wanted to die.

"Have you young women engaged in carnal relations with each other?"

"No, Ma'am," we answered in unison.

Dean Potts removed her glasses. The frame left a red imprint on the bridge of her nose. Without hesitation, she asked the next shaming question, "Have you kissed each other in ways women aren't meant to kiss?"

"No, Ma'am!"

She pointed at each of us in turn, "You two aren't parrots. Answer my questions separately." She turned toward Cindy. "Are you in love with each other?"

"Absolutely not!" Cindy spoke in a cool, steady voice.

Potts looked over at me. "No, Ma'am." Fear vibrated in my words, weakening the denial.

She took a long drag on her cigarette and glanced down at some notes.

"Are you girls currently dating young men?"

"Oh, yes, Ma'am," Cindy jumped in. "I'm pinned to Donald Peters. He's a ZBT." Her face glowed. In that moment, I hated her.

"And you, Joan? Are you involved with a young man?" She seemed to be enjoying the details.

"Yes, Ma'am." I felt queasy. "I'm going steady with David Goldman, a law student who also does the campus radio show." I noticed my arms were leaving blotchy sweat marks on the table.

"I know David. A fine young man!" She squished out her cigarette and jotted something down on a notepad. "Have you told him about this hearing?"

"No Ma'am, I'm too ashamed of these accusations. I don't want to lose him." I figured that sounded pretty normal. *Please God, don't let her contact him!*

"And you, Cindy, have you told your young man about this meeting?"

"No, Ma'am, I'd rather die than tell Don about these awful lies." She looked Dean Potts in the eye. "Joan and I are best friends, that's all!"

Dean Potts read her next question, "Do either of you know of a reason why Charise Motsky would tender a statement accusing you of such behavior?"

"I have a hunch, Ma'am," my voice cracked mid-sentence. "Yes, what is it, Joan?" She stared at me, grabbing her pen again.

"A while back, Charise asked me to be her roommate next September. I refused because we weren't even friends. I had no idea it would hurt her so badly."

"These allegations would be a very unusual reaction to such a slight, Joan." She dropped the pen back on the table with a sharp click, her head swiveling in the direction of Miss Blake. "Do you have any questions for these girls, Miss Blake?"

"No, Dr. Potts, I'm satisfied you've covered all the salient points." She patted Brenda's golden head. She seemed eager to wind things up.

"We will contact you with our decision," Dean Potts rose from her chair. "Oh, I understand you both see school counselors. Please sign these releases so we can obtain further information from them." My hand shook, I stood for a second staring at my signature, certain it revealed my guilt.

"Fine. You girls may go."

Unsteady legs carried me from the conference room. I pushed open the heavy mahogany doors and plunged into the frigid Michigan morning air, filling my lungs to keep from fainting. Cindy followed. Snowflakes settled on our faces. We stared at each other in silence.

So this was the witch trial. We were alive, but barely. Then I sensed another terror.

"Cindy, does your counselor know about us?"

"Do you think I'm that dumb?" Her voice took on a shrill tone. "And what little secrets have you told Dr. Larsen about us?"

"Nothing," I whispered. "Keep your voice down, they're still inside. Honestly, I never discussed us. I was too ashamed. Only some nonsense about Dave."

Cindy's hunched shoulders relaxed, but her eyes burned with the eerie incandescence of a hunted tigress.

***

The next morning I stomped through the snow across campus to the psychology building. Dr. Larsen's office was a cubicle with a wooden desk and two metal chairs. He seemed preoccupied at the start of our session. I assumed he'd received a call from Dean Potts.

"Joan, why didn't you tell me about this problem?"

I avoided his eyes while trying to ignore the shivers rippling through my body. "Doctor, this whole mess was too humiliating to talk about."

He empathized. "Of course, anyone would feel humiliated by such an outrageous accusation."

"You're very kind, Dr, Larsen," I forced the right words.

"Well, there are a few things we have to get out of the way. Let me ask you directly, Joan, have you ever experienced orgasm?"

What? I squirmed. How to answer? "Yes" might make me appear slutty, "no" might suggest a lack of interest in boys. I quickly changed the subject to my weekend with Dave. Why would this balding middle-aged man ask me such things? I'd never trusted him completely.

Then, out of nowhere, he began rattling off unbelievable information about Charise Motsky.

"Joan, this is really not fair to you. There would have been no way for you to know Charise had been seeing a colleague of mine to deal with her latent homosexuality. She'd projected her carnal desire onto Cindy, thereby imagining you and Cindy to be lovers."

I didn't understand the stuff about "projection," but I knew this was a lucky break for me.

"Don't worry Joan, the Dean will decide in your favor." Dr. Larsen ended the session and restarted my heart. My future wasn't ruined; my parents wouldn't find out. I would go free!

But how many people were going to know my business? *No one has any privacy around here, not* even *Charise, that worm.* Maybe Dr. Larsen had been duped, but the girls in the dorm knew. *I'm ruined here anyway.*

Well, there was still Cindy. *If they don't expel us, maybe we could room together next semester.* But Cindy hadn't been going to class. She'd flunk out for sure. Well, then I would follow her to Philadelphia. I'd be a waitress. I'd do anything to be near her.

A month later, Miss Blake sent for me and Cindy in the cafeteria. "Girls we've reached a decision. I'd like to see you in my room when you've finished breakfast."

I ran to the bathroom and lost my bacon and eggs. Cindy held a cold paper towel to my forehead. "Don"t fall apart now, Joanie. You've held us together this far. I need you, no matter what."

"I love you, Cindy."

"Hush," she murmured, "anyone could walk in."

***

We rapped lightly on Miss Blake's door.

"Come in, girls. Please, sit anywhere. The room must be a mess."

"No, it's just fine," said Cindy, her voice a bit raspy.

"Where's Dean Potts?" I asked, relieved not to see her.

"She's out of town but felt this matter should be resolved immediately."

I sat on the floor at Miss Blake's feet, next to Brenda. I

would've changed places with that dog in a second. No one would ever accuse her of being unnatural.

Miss Blake spoke solemnly. "I'm sorry about all of this, girls, but it's the responsibility of the administration to protect the student body."

It's over. I'm finished.

"After an extensive investigation of the evidence, Dr. Potts and I have found you both innocent of all charges." *What did she say?* "No further action will be taken; the matter is dropped. Dean Potts and I apologize for causing you distress."

We thanked her politely and left the room, racing for the empty dorm library. Cindy sat mute in a chair, nose pressed against the windowpane, looking far beyond the frozen trees. I sprawled on the leather sofa and stared up at the tiny holes in the acoustical ceiling. There were no tears left. Only shame.

Finals week had arrived, and I hadn't opened a book the entire semester. I stayed awake for 72 hours, consuming six required texts. At last I could memorize and focus, now that I wasn't a convicted homosexual.

***

Somehow I got through my exams. Nearly unconscious from cramming, I emptied my closet into a trunk for the journey home. Cindy, Dave and I had planned to take the train together from Michigan to Chicago, where Cindy and Dave would continue East. We had all agreed to meet at the Harcourt station.

Cindy didn't show up.

Dave and I waited until the last minute to board the Chicago-bound train.

"She probably got into a fight with Don and forgot the time. She'll catch up with us in Chicago."

"She's always on time. You don't know her the way I do!" I argued, as Dave grabbed two seats near a window. My stomach turned over as the train lurched forward. Placid fields of corn flew by while Dave chatted about his summer plans. I listened, distracted, trying to recapture my last conversation with Cindy.

A mountain of suitcases had covered every inch of hallway in Butler early that morning. Margaret and Joyce had clasped me in a giant bear hug.

"Oh, Joanie, we'll miss you. See you in September!"

I'd rushed to Cindy's room. She sat cross-legged on the floor in her pink nightgown, casually folding cashmere sweaters.

"Why aren't you packed? It's getting late!"

"It's only 8 o'clock, what's the rush?"

"You know Dave is picking us up at 9."

She ran a hand through her disheveled hair. "Last night, Don said he wanted to take me to the station so I'm going with him."

"What? We planned this a week ago."

"Don't worry, Joanie," she looked up into my eyes, "I'll be there at 9:45. Wait for me."

***

Dave and I sat on a bench in Chicago's Union Station for three hours. We waited until all the Harcourt trains had emptied their passengers. I paced the platform. No face escaped scrutiny.

Cindy had vanished.

I saw Dave off on his train to Boston and took a taxi home. He promised to write and visit me every weekend. I knew he would keep his word, but I could only think about Cindy.

Late that night I phoned her home. "But operator, I know this is the right number. Richard Kramer, in Philadelphia. Can't you look it up again?"

"No. That number has been permanently disconnected, and there is no forwarding number."

"That's impossible!" I shouted into the phone. "When was it disconnected?"

"Stop yelling at me, Miss! We don't have that information."

The long-distance operator had been my last hope. Desperate, I mailed Cindy a note:

Dearest Cindy,

Are you all right? Why weren't you at the train? The operator told me your line was disconnected, and I've been so worried. I hope this note reaches you. Please send me your new phone number as soon as possible. I think we could get off-campus housing for next semester. I need to hear the sound of your voice.
Your Joanie.

A few weeks later, I received a postcard.

Dear Joanie,

I'm sorry I missed you at the train. I never intended to hurt you. My family has moved from this address, and I'm going to work next semester because I flunked everything. Take care of yourself. Long letter will follow.
Love, Cindy

5 The Sure Cure

veryone said Saint John University was really tough. *These people are too smart for me. As soon as I open my mouth, they'll know what a phony I am.*

As I walked into the large auditorium filled with rows of eager faces, I longed for the intimacy of the classes at Harcourt. *Intimacy and Harcourt.* I had to force myself to forget it. Here was my present. September, a new start, a new college. Everywhere kids were laughing; they all seemed to know each other. A cute young man smiled at me from the first row.

I took an aisle seat in the center of the auditorium and pulled out the folding desk from the arm of my chair. A familiar voice pierced the chatter, " That's Joanie Lazlow. Isn't she pretty?"

I took a discreet look back. A wave of revulsion shot up my spine. Charise Motsky! *What have I done to deserve this?* The instructor became a blur, his words an indecipherable language.

After class, I made my way down the tiered steps of the lecture hall to the door. Charise was inching her way toward me. I slipped out as the exiting crowd obscured her view.

Outside, the cute young man from the front row leaned against a marble column, smiling. His pale boyish face and curly mop of golden hair caught the sun as he sized me up. His barrel chest and broad shoulders reminded me of my dad. He gave me a grin, but it would be two more weeks before we spoke.

He was lounging on the fender of a '59 Chevy, as I left the elevated train platform at my usual time.

"Hey there, Joan, remember me?"

"Of course, Shakespeare class. You sit in the first row, right? How do you know my name?" *Oh my God, he probably talked to Charise, and now he knows everything.*

"Marty, the teaching assistant told me." He opened the door. "How about a lift home?"

"So what's the address, Joan?" I slid closer to the door, putting as much room between us as possible. I was getting a little scared now that I was in the car. *He's virtually a stranger. How could he know what time I come by?*

"It seems odd you'd be waiting on this corner at 9:30 at night," my frown deepened, "were you just driving by? I don't even know your name."

"It's Roy, Roy Stone, and it wasn't a coincidence," he chuckled to himself. "Actually," he turned red, " I've followed you for a couple of days after class and sort of arranged this accidental meeting."

For a moment I felt a pang of fear, but there was something boyish in the flustered look on his face. I began to relax and tried to hide the smile pulling at the corners of my mouth. We drove a few blocks in silence until he parked in the driveway of my red-brick colonial home in Peterson Park.

"So! You're rich as well as pretty," he winked. The word pretty made me cringe. I thought of Charise. "Say, Joan, do you date boys?"

There it was. *He's here to taunt me. Charise told him everything.*

"Yes, Paul, I date boys." I braced for the dreaded indictment.

"Well, how about a phone number? I went to a lot of trouble to meet you by accident."

I giggled, relieved by his innocence. It was exactly the quality that had been lacking in my life of late. "You're very nice, Roy, and this accidental meeting is flattering, but I'm going steady with somebody from my old school." *Aren't you the paragon of virtue, Joan Lazlow. What a joke!*

"Boy, that's disappointing." Roy draped himself over the steering wheel. "Is it serious?"

I just smiled.

***

Dave had continued to court me long distance. He'd visited me at home every weekend while finishing Harcourt Law School. Debonair Dave, every inch a Perry Mason in his pinstriped black overcoat with matching black fedora, caused mom to flit around the living room, gushing like a schoolgirl. She even presented him with a candy dish of her famous chocolate-covered rum balls. I hated rum.

"How nice of you, Mrs. Lazlow. You know they're my favorite."

"You may call me Miriam, we're hardly strangers. Dave, you look more handsome than a model in a Brooks Brothers catalogue."

"If I'm to be seen with women like you and Joanie, I'd better look good, hadn't I?" He smiled in that devilish way that drove women crazy.

This was turning my stomach. *Maybe she should just divorce Dad and marry Dave; she's obviously flipped over him. Why should I go on with this? I don't need a steady boyfriend to show off anymore. I'll pretend I'm sick.* But it was too late. Dave was holding my coat.

Miriam flushed as Dave brushed by her chair. Irv stood with his hands on his hips and shot him a caustic look. "You lawyers sure know how to flatter the girls."

"Well, you had the good taste to marry a beautiful woman who produced a lovely daughter." He continued smiling in his confident way. Irv found it irritating.

"I don't have a comeback for that, Dave." He was biting his tongue; he had words for Dave all right. The poor guy was trying to score points with the folks, but his easy, sophisticated manner and high-fashion clothes made my dad think that Dave was a show-off.

I needed to release him into the arms of a woman who could love him the way he deserved. I'd never met a more masculine yet sensitive man. He was the best a man could be. The best any girl could want. Why couldn't I be that girl? My head began to ache as I agonized over it for the millionth time.

Whenever Dave turned the conversation to Cindy, I cringed. "Do you miss her? Why do you suppose she doesn't write?" He knew that I'd heard nothing since her note.

"She's just a spoiled brat," he'd say. "Let me track her down. Lawyers have ways of finding people." Why was he nosing into my life? *Mind your own business!* would be on the tip of my tongue, but "Thanks, Dave" dripped from my lips, and I'd lie, "She doesn't matter to me anymore."

One evening, he described an abnormal psychology lecture he'd heard at school.

"Ya know, it's real normal for college kids to develop friendships they mistake for love." He spoke in an earnest tone that frightened me. Why was he bringing this up?

"Really?" I responded with studied indifference while adjusting the hem of my dress. Had he heard the gossip from Butler Hall? Was this his oblique way of saying he knew everything?

If so, it didn't stop him from his intent to map his future with me. One evening right after he'd graduated from law school, Dave was particularly talkative. My folks were out playing bridge, and I was pouring him a Coke, when he dropped the bomb, "Joanie, I guess I should take both bar exams: Massachusetts and Chicago."

"Why? You'll be practicing in Boston."

"Or maybe we'll settle down here in Chicago. Anywhere would be a good town with you by my side." *This is it. The life I've always wanted is right here for the taking. All I need do is reach out and accept the prosperous, normal life that my folks would die for me to have.*

I sighed, my chest heaved. I studied my cuticles to hide my sorrow. I fought to find a voice. "It's best that you only take the Massachusetts bar, Dave."

"You don't want to marry me, Joanie? Is that what you're saying!" Dave's handsome face twitched.

I looked into his warm blue eyes. Everything I'd wanted for a secure life was shrinking away, and my words were doing it.

"I'm not ready for marriage. I may never get married." I shocked myself with the truth.

"I wanted to build a family with you, Joanie. I was hoping we were on the same track."

I took his hand. My voice cracked. "I care deeply for you, Dave, but I haven't found my track yet." I really wanted to want him. I was starting to cry.

"But we've been serious about each other for two years, at least I thought we were." He slouched in an oversized armchair. "I love you, Joanie. I have from the moment I first looked into your eyes."

I couldn't speak anymore.

"Are you sure, Joanie?"

"Yes, I'm sure." I wasn't sure of anything except that I'd lost him forever, and I felt like dying. He was my only true friend. *Dave, you've no idea how much I'll miss you.*

***

The next afternoon, Miriam and I sat together in the den. She was sewing a hem on my new pedal pushers.

"Ma, Dave asked me to marry him."

"Wonderful! Finally! Wait 'til I tell your father!"

"Don't get excited; I refused him." Miriam's face dropped into her coffee cup. The sewing box slipped from her lap to the floor, colorful buttons and pins pirouetting across the parquet.

"You'd have to be an idiot not to want him!" Her face was expanding like a red balloon. I hoped she'd float out the window.

"Because I'm not in love with him!" I coughed back tears.

"You're not in love with him," she mimicked me. "So you'll learn to love him."

"Did you learn to love Daddy?"

Ma looked away, "No it was at first sight with Irv. But I was only 16."

"Why do you want less for me?"

She was crawling under the furniture, searching out scattered buttons and pins. She sat back, legs folded beneath her and paused, staring at the handfuls of spools clutched in her lap. "I've always wanted the best for you, Joan. David is the best. I can't understand why you won't do one good thing for yourself."

I finished my senior year at Saint John University. Charise and I never exchanged a word. David had left and Cindy was gone. Nothing seemed to matter anymore.

***

"Anything from Pennsylvania, Joe?" I greeted the postman every morning at 9, hoping for the promised long letter from Cindy that never arrived.

"No, Joan, I'm sorry. That guy on the Coast must be some special beau, huh?"

"Guess I'm not that special, that's the problem."

"Wait and see, he'll write."

Don't worry, Joanie, I'll be there at 9:45. Wait for me.

***

Six months passed. I was in despair, but I was afraid to slit my wrists, even though I'd read in *Photoplay* magazine that it was the popular style of suicide among movie stars. Too bloody! I'd checked out the bathroom cabinet, but discovered only Bayer aspirin and a bottle of Midol. I didn't want to live without Cindy, but I couldn't figure out how to die.

Maybe I could try psychoanalysis. I'd read it was a miracle cure. Ingrid Bergman cured Gregory Peck from amnesia in *Spellbound*, and I'd love an analyst like Ingrid Bergman. Even Gregory Peck wouldn't be bad. I'd hated my psychologist at

Harcourt, but he wasn't a real doctor. Only a real medical doctor could help me overcome my affliction.

I couldn't manage another day of sleepwalking with this brick inside my chest. One morning I sat daydreaming at our Formica kitchen table in my striped pajamas and bobby socks, talking with Miriam while she rinsed out breakfast dishes. Ma scrubbed clean every plate and pan, because the automatic dishwasher couldn't be trusted.

"Ma, I need to see a psychiatrist right away," I blurted out.

"Why? You're not crazy." Without missing a beat, her rubber-gloved hands seized another pot.

"Ma, look at me."

Annoyed, she turned in my direction. "I'm looking, now what?"

"Ma, what would you say if I told you I was a homosexual?" My confession blasted like a gunshot.

"I'd say you kids in college try everything." She turned back to the dishes. She didn't want to hear it.

I picked up a spoon and threw it in her direction. It missed her head, careened into the sink, and smashed some glasses. Miriam lunged for the phone. Was she calling the police?

"Irv! Come home right away! Joan just attacked me! She's out of her head. She's saying outrageous things! No, I can't repeat the things. Stop joking, Irv. What do you mean, how did she attack me? She threw a spoon at me!"

Immediately following the "spoon incident," Miriam phoned our physician, who referred me to Henry Marx, M.D., a specialist in the problems of young people. I became a full-fledged patient of Dr. Henry Marx, a graduate of the Chicago Psychoanalytic Institute.

Dr. Marx's office was small but serious looking. He sat behind an enormous mahogany desk, complete with a framed picture of Sigmund Freud. Reclined on the couch, eyes shut, I pretended my heavyset savior was Dr. Gregory Peck. But he wasn't.

"Joan, I understand your sexual confusion. It's common in the young. Within months you'll be a normal, well-adjusted young lady."

Could it be true? If so, I was very lucky to have found him. My folks agreed to pay for the analysis until I found a job. Ma didn't want another spoon assault.

6 A Man For All Reasons

I lay on Dr. Marx's couch trying to free associate. I was sick of taking the Michigan Avenue bus to his office four times a week. Student-teaching history, then analysis. What a life! When was I going to get cured?

Dr Marx spoke in his "know-it-all" voice from behind the couch, "My dear, don't worry. You are definitely not a lesbian. I know what lesbians look like. I've been in practice for years. You are much too feminine. What's going on here is that you have confused your dependency needs with your sexual needs. It's very common with young people."

I felt both relieved and betrayed by his words. Relieved that an expert had diagnosed me as normal, and betrayed because he didn't really know me. *Is it sick to be dependent on someone you love?*

* * *

After one of my Friday evening sessions with Dr. Marx, I joined my cousin Suzie to hear a lecture on the Hungarian Revolt, by her fiancé Franz.

It was a frigid evening. We all huddled in the drab, unheated auditorium like displaced refugees. *Damn, why am I here? This is stupid, I should be home grading papers. It's cold, my life is boring, there's no reason to...wow, who is that hunk of a guy up there on the stage?* I looked in awe at his hazel eyes. There was something hard and sad in them. *He's seen things I've never seen, been places I'll never go.* Beneath his shirt and jacket was a rock-solid physique, the shoulders and chest of a man who'd known his share of battle.

"Get a load of the Adonis with the black, wavy hair!" I said to Suzy. "He could be a movie star."

"Oh, I know him," she whispered. "I guess I never noticed, but he's kind of cute if you like dark types."

Suzie's golden-haired fiancé continued to speak about the horrors of Stalin, but my Greek god uttered not a word. Handsome and mysterious, he peered out with militant severity.

Finally, Franz introduced him, "Good friends, the young man on my right is Anton Densonovitz, one of the bravest freedom fighters of the Hungarian Revolt. He escaped from prison and made his way alone to the United States."

"Suzie, how did Franz meet him?" I was breathless, and I wanted details.

"He's Franz's roommate, a real-live hero, but his English is rough. Anton rescued an entire schoolhouse of children from Soviet gunfire."

An entire schoolhouse of children!

After the presentation, I charged through the crowd, dragging Suzie behind me to introduce us. Wasn't he a hero like Anne Frank? He was, in fact, a hero who'd risen from the ashes.

Suzie hugged Franz and introduced Anton, whose gold-speckled hazel eyes remained glued to a blonde in the first row. I felt something flutter in the pit of my stomach—a longing. A sexual longing for a man, unbelievable! For the first time in my life, I was physically attracted to a guy. Of course, the guy didn't know I existed. I didn't care. I'd catch him. Dr Marx was right. I was normal! That wavy black hair and those hazel eyes. They weren't for me yet, but all I needed was time.

That night I raced upstairs to my folks' bedroom and burst in.

"Guess what? I'm getting married!"

"That's nice, Joanie, go to sleep." Dad was in a daze.

"He's a hero, a Hungarian freedom fighter."

"Is he Jewish?" Ma managed that one through a yawn.

"Yes."

"I don't trust foreigners, including Jewish ones. Why didn't you want Dave? He was a nice, decent American boy."

"Dave puts on airs. Joanie wants someone down to earth," mumbled Dad.

"Down to earth? Irv, you're a card. Everyone knows foreigners are big wolves and bad providers."

"So glad you're happy for me," I called over my shoulder on my way to bed. "I knew you would be. Thanks for listening."

"Irv, Joan's being snotty," Miriam raised her voice to be sure I'd hear.

"Really, you could have fooled me," Irv stage-whispered. "Let's go to sleep everybody!"

***

For several days following our meeting, I imagined Anton would call, but he didn't. *What's wrong with him? I'm sure Suzie told him I was interested.* I wasn't used to being ignored by men. I didn't like it one bit. I picked up the phone.

"Hello?"

"Suzie, it's Joanie,"

"Oh, hi Joanie. Is something wrong?"

"Not really, remember that guy, the gorgeous Hungarian? What gives?"

"Oh, Anton. He's seeing a blonde named Arlene. He's not interested in you, I asked him You'd better give up. It won't do you any good to moon over him." The last part took on a nasty singsong quality that made me even more determined.

Nice girls didn't phone boys, so I needed an excuse, and it had to be couched in an innocent motive. Suzie provided the phone number.

"Hi, Anton, you probably don't remember me. My name is Joan Lazlow, I met you at Franz's lecture.

"Yes," he said. And that's all he said.

I froze. I started to drop the receiver and juggled it from hand to hand, trying to keep it from hitting the table. I began talking nonstop. "I'd-really-like-to-hear-more-about-the-

Hungarian-Revolution-and-you-won't-believe-this-but-some-
one-gave-me-two-free-tickets-to-a-Maria-Callas-concert-
next-Saturday-night——

Would you like to be my guest?...You don't, well...But she's a famous opera star....Oh, you haven't seen opera....She's the greatest singer in the world....Yes, really!...So you'll come?"

His lack of enthusiasm infuriated me.

"Would you like my address and phone number?"

"Yes, let me find paper," he mumbled.

***

I was delighted with the Callas concert, but Anton displayed more interest in the baroque architecture of the opera house than in Maria's magnificent voice. At dinner he talked about himself. He didn't ask any personal questions. What a relief after Dave!

"Ya, I will soon be 29 years. Much older than you, hum? This is problem? I work days keeping books for my uncle in fur business downtown. Nighttime, I study for accounting master's degree. If I keep to hard work, I take CPA test in two years. But time pass fast, you think?"

His European accent sounded charming. It reminded me of Otto Frank and Amsterdam. I smiled and nodded at the appropriate pauses, keeping my eyes glued seductively on his, "Anton, you are an amazing self-made man, the most ambitious guy I've ever met."

"Oh, not true," he blushed. The next day he phoned for a date. *Blondie, you don't have a chance!*

Here was a guy who didn't pry into my world. The surface pleased him. My past was of no significance. I was a nice educated girl from a nice, middle-class family. Why should he suspect skeletons in my closet?

Other girls might have considered Anton a great-looking rock of a man but, like me, he was protecting his mushy insides from pain. I guarded against being exposed and hid from the shame of my college past. Anton steeled himself against awful memories of seeing his buddies slaughtered in the streets of Budapest.

Although Dave had been the perfect catch, he'd invaded my murky world.

"Joanie, I'm not hero," Anton confided in me one evening while we kissed in the car. "The thought of torture by Russian soldiers scared me so much that I like to die better from jumping out of prison window."

His confession touched me. I imagined his sweet face smudged with gunpowder, hurling grenades at tanks.

"I hated those soldiers. Each one was a Hitler. Nighttime, I see them coming. Shadows on the wall moving. I see my friends' faces blown up to bits. Nothing mattered to us but freedom. We never thought about death, then. But the battle was lost. We lost." His hazel eyes softened and watered over.

"You're a brave man, Anton. I'm proud of you." I cradled his head in my arms. "You're a hero to me." I'd seen no sign of the fury that must have burst from his heart during those times. I was filled with sadness and wonder that he'd give his life for an ideal.

My dates with Anton included some intimacy in the tiny, third-floor walk-up apartment he shared with Franz. Always proper and polite, Franz phoned before he arrived, so as not to invade our romantic interludes. Anton would do the same when Franz and Suzie were together.

I enjoyed making out with him within limits. It felt wonderful to be held, kissed and fondled. Little did he know he was only caressing the padding of my *Peter Pan Hidden Treasure Bra*.

Eventually, an inexplicable urge overwhelmed me. I allowed Anton to reach beneath my panties, and bring me to orgasm with his hand. Where and how I'd first experienced that thrill was my darkest secret. It was the early '60s, America hadn't yet entered the Age of Aquarius and the Sexual Revolution. It was important that my virginity remain intact, at least as far as he was concerned.

Anton broached the question one night after a necking session in his apartment. "Some couples go all the way before marriage. What do you think, Joanie?" He avoided my eyes as he punched up the sofa pillows.

"I believe in staying a virgin until marriage," I lied.

"That's what I love about you. You are a very moral girl, the kind my mama would love."

I was ashamed of lying to such an innocent, honest man. It was getting harder to live with myself with every lie. But it was what Dr. Marx ordered me to do. It was part of the cure.

A few of my friends actually admitted to having sex with their fiancé—and only their fiancé—before marriage. Certainly it was possible to take the pill and have sex; it wasn't fear that kept me from sexual intercourse, but no urge compelled me toward it.

I began having weird, disappointing dreams about Cindy. She appeared, not just fat, but enormous. Was I unconsciously trying to blot her out? After three years of making out in Anton's apartment, I still felt an emotional emptiness. It was satisfying and sweet, but not raging and torrid like it was with Cindy. Had danger been the attraction with her? After all, there were no risks with Dave or Anton. Did I just enjoy living on the edge? Ridiculous! No one feared discovery more. I'd despised the intrigue, the humiliation and shame. Yet I missed those savage, out-of-control feelings.

One evening, my frustration took over, and I blurted out, "Anton, maybe something's wrong with me; there are no bells and whistles when we kiss!"

"You American girls believe all the romantic nonsense you see in movies," he laughed. "Real ladies do not like sex. Mama told me this long time ago, and she would know."

His comment disturbed and soothed me at the same time. Though I'd longed for handsome Anton to sweep away all thoughts of Cindy, he wouldn't pressure a girl into going all the way.

Intercourse would wait until our wedding night. And for Anton it was an unspoken certainty that that day would come.

Cindy and I had whispered softly throughout our love-making, but Anton and I maneuvered in silence. Maybe love talk was a girl thing.

In time, our necking grew heavy. Anton claimed to have had lots of experience with women, so when he asked for oral sex I assumed it was a normal enough thing to do.

***

"Is this really okay with you, Joanie? Some women don't like it."

It was exciting to experience his muscular body tensing and relaxing under my influence. It felt good to evoke such a profound response from this powerful man. "Well, honey, you found a woman who likes it." I ran my fingers through his black wavy hair.

One evening, while lying together in bed, Anton kissed my eyelids. "Joanie, you have a tenderness I have not known before. I love your mouth. Soft. And your hands, so delicate. Am I a fool to think about you every moment?"

Are you a fool, Anton? Maybe, I don't know. Cindy's voice echoed through the years, "you're a wonderful lover, Joanie…"

Once Anton tried to bury his head in my curly muff, but I pushed him away. "No honey, not now. I need a shower." Only Cindy's lips could know that spot.

Sometimes I felt jealous of Anton's pleasure, his ecstasy was so much more profound. Maybe his Hungarian mama was right about sex. But I'd loved it with Cindy. I'd loved everything with Cindy.

I worked constantly to deny the memory of my body exploding from the sight of her. My thoughts inevitably drifted back to her rain forest scent and that overwhelming need.

***

A few days later, I returned to Dr. Marx. He interrupted my lamenting the loss of Cindy about halfway into the session.

"We've heard enough about your girlfriend. Tell me about the man in your life, you never talk about Anton."

Marx figured Cindy had probably married and forgotten all about me by now. Had it really been three years?

"Joan, you must concentrate your thoughts on Anton. Marriage is the sure cure for this lapse in your development."

I sat up on the couch and looked Marx in the eye. "Would you want to be called Mrs. Anton Densonovitz?" Dr. Marx cleared his throat.

"If the name bothers you, ask him to change it. Doesn't he want to be a real American?"

***

The doctor positively beamed, the day I presented my 1.25-karat engagement ring. "Congratulations! Very sweet. I'm sure Anton will replace it as soon as his fortunes increase."

Why would he put down my engagement ring? Wasn't it the symbol of a successful analysis? I'd thought the ring beautiful and far more extravagant than Anton could afford.

Perhaps Dr. Marx believed I deserved better because he thought of me as a sort of movie star patient. He often said I looked like Dolores del Rio. Who the hell was Dolores del Rio? What could anyone expect from such an old man? He had to be at least 45.

***

I immediately put the subject of actually getting married out of my mind. I'd broken through in analysis, wasn't that enough? No, not enough for Anton. One snowy Friday in February he caught me on the steps of Marshall High after class. Judging from his somber expression, something was up. That something was the marriage license. He spoke through a stony stare.

"Joanie, I think I know the reason you are not excited to marry me." My heart froze. I stopped breathing.

"What makes you say that?" *God help me, he knows. He found out everything.*

"It is one month since we get engaged. You act like all is the same as before. I think you meet another man."

I exhaled and flicked the snowflakes off his coal-black hair.

"How can you think such a thing? There's no man for me but you. Why the rush, after all we're engaged?"

"Joanie, our license expires today."

"We can get another."

Anton's patience had reached its limit. "I will not have one more delay tactic. Marry me today. Now, or you never again will see my face!"

I ran across the street into a drugstore to phone my parents, while Anton waited in the car. "Hi, Ma, it's me. I gotta get married this afternoon...no, I'm not pregnant....No, I don't want a big wedding...Ma, no, I'm not pregnant, I swear!...I'll explain later. You and dad meet me at the courthouse on Huron Street in half an hour. See you there!"

The blinding snow was already blanketing the parked cars. I sprinted across the street to Anton's blue Ford. My knees were red and raw from running through the icy cold, the passenger seat was freezing against my legs. As I blew into my hands, Anton reached out and warmed them between his strong palms. Seconds later, he took a small box from the glove compartment.

"Joanie, I have been thinking of this and only this for weeks." He opened a tiny black case containing the wedding band to my engagement ring.

"Wow! That's beautiful." I loved it. I really loved it. Why couldn't I keep the ring and forget about the marriage?

Miriam, Irv, Anton and I sat like mannequins in the wood-paneled anteroom of Judge O'Connor's chambers. A radiant couple sat opposite us. Their happy faces made me sick. I began pacing back and forth like a prisoner on death row. Like an assembly-line worker, the judge pieced together one little marriage after another. I kept ignoring his prompt of,

"Next couple!" while Miriam and Irv stared straight ahead in embarrassed silence.

After a few couples, he announced he would be leaving at 5:30.

"Now, Joanie? We go or no?" Anton hissed.

"Okay, I'm ready." My enthusiasm rivaled that of Anne Boleyn at the block, as I folded my coat and gathered my purse to hand to Miriam.

"Are your witnesses present?" I winced at the voice of the rotund silver-haired judge.

"Uh! Yes!" I gestured half-heartedly at Miriam who looked at me with sadness, her lap spilling over with my stuff.

"Well, fine, let's get on with it. A handsome couple indeed."

I felt faint from the pressure of Anton's wary eye and the stifling heat of the room. The ceremony took about the time necessary to make a hard-boiled egg. An officer of the court whisked us out as quickly as we'd been ushered inside, the marriage factory closed for the day.

Shivering from the wind blasts ripping off the lake, our bridal party trudged through snowy, slushy streets, back to the parking lot as if nothing changed. Miriam and Irv got into the front seat of the car, and I slid into the back. My new husband stood alone on the curb, stunned.

"Joanie, aren't you in the wrong car?" Dad glanced over his shoulder.

"No, please, let's go! I promised to marry him, and I did." I was near tears. "Please, Dad, I want to go home *now!*"

"Leave her alone, Irv, what's the rush? Joan's obviously not ready to live with him," said Miriam.

"Rush? How many years have you been going with Anton, Joan?" Irv was trying not to laugh. "What about a wedding night or a honeymoon?"

"Stop it, Irv." Miriam was emphatic. "Not every girl has ants in her pants. If Anton loves her, he'll wait." Thank God for Ma! I could never figure her out.

The phone was ringing the moment we got home. "What's going on, Joanie?"

"I'm not ready," I pleaded. It all happened too fast.

"But we're married," he persisted.

"I don't want to talk about it now." I hung up and collapsed on the sofa.

He phoned again the next morning.

"Anton, I need time to get used to this. Can't we wait until we get a place of our own?"

"All right, Joanie, it makes sense, but this weekend we look for apartment."

"You are a very understanding, uh, uh, husband." An unbelievable word. Relieved, I returned to my bedroom. Neither of us had suggested a honeymoon. Consummation could wait.

Even though I'd refused to leave home, my parents gave us wedding presents. I shoved the beautiful silver and china gifts into the closet. Shopping for apartments with Anton would be bittersweet; I'd never let go of my plan to share a place with Cindy. I still hated how everything had fallen apart for us.

Don't be ridiculous! Girls aren't couples in the real world!

Time was running out so quickly. How wretched to leave the soothing familiarity of my old room with prom souvenirs and storybook dolls. None of this could come along into the home of a grown-up woman, a married woman.

We found a charming apartment. I had to admit it was nice. I actually enjoyed furnishing our new home. We had the latest Danish teak furniture and brass lamps. A framed, wide-eyed Keane orphan hung over the sofa. She was like a hidden part of me, staring out from her lonely world.

***

"Well, honey, this is it!" Whatever "it" meant. Anton turned the key of our new apartment and swung the door open. I stepped across the threshold so he wouldn't try to carry me over, and I looked around.

"Our new home is ready for occupancy," he smiled. There was a hopeful note in his voice. He certainly had been patient.

Later that night we crawled into our new bed. By now his hands on me had become a familiar, pleasant sensation, but this time was different. There was a determination steering his touch.

I knew he had a goal in mind. Foreplay was secondary, Anton was ready for the main event. I held my breath while he parted my legs and began to thrust. I wrenched in pain and begged him to stop.

"Honey, I'm sorry!" He pulled back, frightened. "Maybe you should see a woman's doctor. Sometime they do a stretch when girls are tiny inside."

Of course, it must be physical. My vagina was too small. A little stretching would do the trick.

"Everything's in place, tip top." Dr. Barnett rose from the table, pelvic exam folder in hand.

"So why does intercourse hurt? Aren't you going to stretch me?"

"No, that's not necessary, Joan. I'll give you a lubricant. But it's important you concentrate on erotic thoughts to stimulate yourself. A woman must take charge of her own lubrication and orgasm.

The medical gook didn't cut the pain. I supplemented with Vaseline. Anton couldn't feel much with all that gook inside me. I felt guilty.

"Joanie, don't worry about me, everything will work out in time. Many girls have this problem at first. Especially virgins."

"You're right, Anton, it's a virgin problem." I desperately wanted to be a normal woman who enjoyed intercourse. On Saturdays while Anton was at work, I secretly experimented with myself to see if I'd dried up. I found that lying alone in bed with memories of Cindy transporting me, I certainly had not. So why couldn't I get aroused with my husband? Maybe I'd try fantasizing about Cindy while making love with Anton.

In bed that night, I went numb. My fantasies seemed disrespectful to Anton, and a defilement of Cindy. Had my analysis failed? Should I go see Dr. Marx? Never!

What could I tell my parents and friends? I'd taken the
right path, shouldn't I be happy like the rest of the girls? They
were *happy* weren't they? Anton didn't mistreat me, and he
was proud to have wrested me from my parents and the arms
of other suitors. I had everything I was supposed to want.

On my 25th birthday, we went to the Empire Room at the
Palmer House Hotel. A gypsy violinist walked among the
tables. At the booth next to ours, he began a tune. Like a familiar perfume, the words wafted through my mind, enveloping
me in Cindy's memory until tears collected in my eyes:

"A song of love is a sad song/ hi Lili, hi Lili, hi lo…" It's
November. We sit, elbows touching, in the dark campus theater. On the screen is a delicate waif, madly in love with a car-
nival magician who spurns her. Her boss, a crippled pup-
peteer, is obsessed with unrequited love for Lili. His desperation drives him to cruelty. Obsession, jealousy, unrequited
love.

*Cindy, with your sapphire eyes and soft olive skin, why
can't I let you go?*

While Anton read the wine list, I stared out at the rain. I
wanted to be bathing in it, cleansed of my past regrets…The
violin played on: "…A song of love is a song of woe/ don't ask
me how I know/ hi Lili, hi Lili, hi lo."

7 The Promised Land

"Mrs. Denson, this is the third time you've been to my office in one week," grumbled my employment supervisor, Mrs. Garfield, "what is it about 'no jobs' that you don't understand?" The icy, stained windows were shut tightly against the wind.

There's no air in here. This woman detests me; she'll never get me a job. I paced her small, drab green office.

"But my guidance counselor said I would have no problem getting a job after graduation. She said there was a shortage of history teachers." I leaned forward, hands outstretched, pleading my case and containing an urge to leap across the desk and grab her by the lapels. "Please, I've been studying for five years. I want to work!"

"Perhaps your guidance counselor was referring to the teacher shortage in Mississippi," snarled Mrs. Garfield. "You are getting on my nerves, young lady!"

"I can't move to Mississippi."

"Mrs. Denson, your specialty is history. There is no work for you in that specialty in Chicago. History is taught by men here, and they don't leave the system, they retire from it. There are lots of kindergarten and first grade positions, however." She avoided my hostile stare.

"I have a degree in history, and you're offering me kindergarten?"

"Lower your voice. Life is rarely fair, young lady. You can substitute teach like everyone else in your boat." She tossed an application on the desk and turned around to her typewriter, growling over her shoulder, "Fill this out, Mrs. Denson, and don't come back until you hear from me."

Kids were terrible to substitutes, and it wasn't steady work, anyway. How would I pay for Dr. Marx?

"Please, Mrs. Garfield, I'm desperate, I have heavy medical bills."

She turned back around to face me. "Really, your file indicates you're in perfect health." The phone interrupted our talk. "Yes?…I'm very sorry to hear that. I'll see what I can do." She hung up and gazed silently out the window. After a few moments, she turned toward me. "It looks like someone else's tragedy may be your good fortune, Mrs. Denson. Unfortunately, Mr. Perkins of Washington High had a heart attack and is leaving his position. That's the inner city. Are you willing to tackle the inner city?" There was a smug edge to her voice.

"I don't care where I teach, so long as I teach history. Kids are kids!"

***

Seven years later, having survived an eye-opening inauguration into the workings of an inner-city school, I stood at my blackboard writing out the next day's history assignment. I drew a big happy face as a punctuation mark. *They'll get a kick out of this.* I'd thrown myself into my work and had finally begun to see results. Though my students brought me a sense of purpose, their success hadn't relieved my emptiness.

At 29, my life is over. I've met Anne Frank's father, seen Europe, been through psychoanalysis, entered my chosen career, and married a nice guy. What a joke! I teach my kids about great people having the courage to change the world, and I struggle each day to keep going. Instead of venturing out to conquer life, I'd covered my head and hidden. To Dr. Marx, I was a success story. Marriage had cured my "identity problem" and earned me the right to vegetate forever.

Saturday afternoon I was still in a funk. The highlight of my week was that day's baby shower. I looked forward to escaping our apartment, with Anton snoring on the sofa while a ballgame droned from the tv.

About 20 young women sat in a circle around Ruthie, as she meticulously unwrapped each gift, careful to save the bow. We "oohed" and "ahhed" in unison over tiny pajamas and pink quilts which would grace the nursery.

Motherhood had transformed my previously savvy colleagues into professors of poo-poo diapers. They researched such Einsteinian theories as diaper relativity.

"My doctor believes that the new disposable *Pampers* are less hygienic than cloth," proclaimed Ruthie, in a strident tone of medical absolutism. "Of course, the diaper service is more costly; but when it comes to the health of my child, expense is not a concern." Her coven of diaper consultants nodded in agreement.

A cucumber sandwich later, I was behind the wheel of my car, navigating a Chicago hailstorm, a soothing contrast to the smothering domestic scene. If babies caused a woman's IQ to plunge, I would have to postpone that part of marriage, too.

At dinner Anton surprised me with: "...and right out of the blue sky, my boss said, 'So, Anton, how would you like to be chief of accounting in our San Francisco office?'"

"And you said?"

"'I'll talk to my wife.' What else?" He beamed at me.

California was the Promised Land for professionals. Maybe it would be my salvation, too.

"Take it, Anton, it's the opportunity of a lifetime. It sounds exciting."

"Joan, you are perfect. Not every wife would leave her home, even to help her husband's career. I clean up tonight; you call your parents and give them the news."

***

Anton's company eased the pain of relocation by hosting us at the Mark Hopkins Hotel for a month. Anton would return each day to a collection of room-service trays outside the door.

"Joan, I see you eat well, but it's not good to hide in de room. This city is beautiful. A walk everyday will make you feel better."

A week later, I worked up the nerve to venture out alone. Fisherman's Wharf, Market Street, The Embarcadero, best of all was the Japanese garden in Golden Gate Park.

I made a ritual of boarding a trolley to my Japanese sanctuary each morning. I loved the serenity and sensuality of its delicately carved bridges, transparent lily ponds and exotic colors. I'd sit for hours listening to the wind rustle through the coral trees. The quiet allowed me to hear myself.

How did I get stuck on a passionless island of a marriage? It happened because I wanted to fit in. *Nobody forced me to make the choice, I'd done it to myself. Now I'm completely isolated with no one but Anton and nothing to do.*

It was actually a relief to admit to myself that I was miserable in San Francisco. I decided to talk to Anton the minute he got home.

"Anton, this move was a mistake. I want to go home."

"You're homesick, honey, it will pass."

"It's better in Chicago," I continued, "the people are more friendly, prices are more reasonable." I started to whine, "Anton, I hate it here."

I'd gone too far, he snapped. "Joan! My career isn't a yo-yo! Just stop complaining! You wanted me to take this job, now have a little patience. You'll adjust!"

I winced at his sudden outburst and glared at my plate.

"I'm sorry, honey, I didn't mean to yell. Why don't you call Dr. Marx, long distance?"

I'd rather die of loneliness.

We started searching immediately for an apartment. After all, a new home had worked the first time. We discovered an elegant bay-view apartment in Pacific Heights. The building faced a lovely private park, but it was off limits to anybody without a pedigree or a special key. From the fourteenth floor, we watched dowagers parading their well-bred canines through a park we'd never seen up close.

One rainy afternoon, as I arranged our books in the den, I discovered my old ragged *The Diary of A Young Girl*. I should write Papa Frank, but so much has happened that I can't tell him. I missed him, but I just couldn't bring myself to write.

I wondered about my dear friend Anne, with whom I'd never spoken. Could I have talked with her about Cindy and me? She believed people were really good at heart. Did that include homos and frauds?

***

I needed a purpose, and decided graduate school would point me in the right direction. On my first evening at the University of San Francisco, a young African-American woman strolled down the aisle to the front of the room. She was barefoot, wore a colorful Mexican poncho and had a small dog trailing behind her.

My God, get me out of here. What kind of class is this? She smirked when she passed my desk, sizing up my Gucci bag, snakeskin loafers and bouffant hairdo. She stopped, did a U-turn over to my desk and took off her glasses. She bit down on the plastic rim. "Hmm, yes, I have a fine research topic for you." The fiendish glint in her eyes was unmistakable. "What's your name?"

"Joan Denson."

She jotted something down on a clipboard. "Yes, Joan, 'Hippies' will be your term paper topic."

The students around me snickered at the bewildered look on my face. "What are hippies?"

"What a square!" A voice called from the back of the room.

"Quiet down," Dr. Barefoot admonished. This will be a great experiment in sociology for…what's your name, again?" She glanced to the clipboard, "Yes, a learning experience for Joan Denson."

That night at dinner I asked Anton if he'd ever heard of the Haight-Ashbury district.

"Ya, that's a terrible place, where all the hippies live. You must never go there, Joan. It's not safe."

"But I have a term paper on hippies for class."

"Good God. What next?"

***

Anton leaned against the bar, sipping his espresso, "How much longer do we stay here? We already have been to three cafes tonight. My employees would think I was nuts if they saw me here."

"But I haven't talked to any hippies."

"Look over there, that guy's on something. Better yet, talk to her, she's a cute hippie."

"How do you know she's a hippie?"

"She's not wearing a bra. Girl hippies don't wear bras."

Now he's a hippie expert—scary looking guys and girls with no bras. I wished I'd left him home.

"What's so special about hippies? They don't work, they are shirkers. Where I come from, if you do not work, you do not eat. Look in their eyes, you can see they are all dope addicts."

I couldn't take his lecture anymore. I wandered down the bar. Just then, a hollow-eyed guy in a tight-fitting T-shirt and tie-dyed jeans stumbled up to Anton. "Hey, man, wanna buy a little Mary Jane?"

Anton hurried over. "Can you imagine that? He's selling his sister to me! These people have no shame! I don't want you here with pimps."

"Do you really think he's a pimp?"

"Of course, I know things. We should not be here, let's go."

"I can't Anton. I have to do interviews." I strolled up to a regular-looking guy. His girlfriend sat across from him, braiding her waist-length blonde hair. Turquoise Indian jewelry adorned every visible inch of her skin.

"Excuse me, I'm Joan, and I'm doing a paper on hippies for San Francisco State. I wonder if I could interview you and your girlfriend."

The long-haired blonde turned toward her boyfriend, "Get a load of this chick."

The young man smiled, revealing a mouth full of yellow, crooked teeth. He brushed me away with a flick of his wrist. "Hey, mellow out!"

So much for peace and love.

I scurried back to Anton and told him what happened. He ordered me a cup of coffee and shrugged his shoulders. "See? I told you, good for nothings."

But I wasn't giving up. Maybe there was some kind of book on the hippie culture I could crib from.

We headed for the Kama Sutra bookstore. As I gazed at the glass display case full of strange paraphernalia, a balding Indian man behind the counter smiled at me, "Welcome to my humble bookstore. May I help you?

I suddenly felt like a foreigner in my own country. "Well, I'm looking for a book…" I hesitated, distracted by silver and jade trinkets in the case. "Sir, what is that?"

Anton whispered, "Let's get out of here. I hate the smell." He was standing next to an incense holder burning at the end of the counter. I ignored him and turned back to the man.

"Oh, that's our finest roach clip. Very fine quality."

"Roach clip? Like a mousetrap for bugs?"

"Where are you two from, my dear?"

"Chicago, I'm studying hippies."

"Yes, I see. Some people use them to smoke…"

"Cigarettes!" I had seen the light.

"Well, no—joints—Mary Jane—marijuana."

I stared at him in wonder. He caressed the ankh around his neck and opened his hand like a mystic, as though creating a pathway between his heart and mine. He reached into his shirt pocket and took out what appeared to be the end of a cigarette.

"Now you understand, Miss," he simulated smoking, "marijuana is very expensive, so we savor every last bit."

"Yes, thank you for the demonstration." My mind whirled

with the shock of seeing pot pulled out in public, while Bob Dylan's voice in the background mumbled about a "simple twist of fate." I couldn't understand the lyrics. I was ready to go.

Anton tapped me on the shoulder. "Can we leave now?"

I put down the roach clip. "Thank you, sir. That book, back there…"

"You don't mind a used book?"

"No, it's fine, I never had a chance to read it."

"Of course, yes, do come by again." He put Kerouac's *On the Road* into a blue *Kama Sutra* paper bag, with the address printed on it. I planned to come again without Anton.

Outside the shop, I saw a group of girls with long straight hair and tie-dyed clown pants. Before I could get out the second line of my term paper interview speech, one of them hissed, "Get lost, man!"

In the car, Anton wiped off his jacket as if dusting away any trace of our recently discovered dens of iniquity. "Why don't you drop that stupid sociology? We should spend our evenings with people like us. We need some normal friends."

"You're right, Anton." I stared out the window, absorbed in thought. *Dr. Barefoot set me up! She knew no one in Haight-Ashbury would talk to me. What a lousy trick!*

Two days later, I went back, this time in a flowing skirt and dangling Navajo earrings (from Neiman Marcus, but who'd know?). By mutual agreement, Anton lingered behind me. His orders were to be protective but unobtrusive.

I saw a likely looking guy resting against a lamppost. His eyes were vacant, and he was thin and unshaven. I sat on a bus-stop bench within his earshot. "Did you hear they're sending another 60,000 to Vietnam?"

"Hey, sister," he looked over, "war is unhealthy for all living things."

For the next hour, we engaged in a disjointed conversation about the war, the *Kama Sutra*, Timothy Leary, Janis Joplin, and the outrageous cost of good grass, during which he made his way to the bench and slid next to me.

"Well, Sebastian," I glanced at an impatient Anton leaning against a wall half a block away, "This was cool. Really cool. I've enjoyed our talk."

Sebastian nodded and rested his arm around the back of the bench. "Hey, chick, what's your name?"

"I told you my name," I lied.

"Oh, yeah, right. Listen, I've got some weed, why don't we go back to my pad and get it on?"

Anton had seen the tattooed arm around my shoulders and closed the half-block distance in about 30 seconds, his eyes hard with rage.

"Joan," he grabbed my arm, "let's go!"

Sebastian jumped up and extended his hand to shake. "Hey, man, I didn't know she was your old lady."

Anton ignored Sebastian's hand and dragged me away to the car, muttering in Hungarian.

As we sped toward home in silence, I heaved a sigh. A part of me envied these kids. They'd found a place to belong.

***

Back in class the next evening, the woman behind me tapped me on the shoulder, "I'm Jasmine. You're Joan, the one with the hippy topic, right? She's a character, don't you think?"

Jasmine was one of the older students in class. I'd noticed her exotic looks the first day but was intimidated by her sophistication.

"Your loafers are Anne Klein, aren't they?" I nodded, as Jasmine gave me an approving look. I glanced down at my feet, then up at her and smiled. I knew I'd found a friend, someone like me.

"Let's have a drink at Angie's Bistro after class."

"Great, I'll meet you there." Anton and I never drank anything but Coca-Cola.

As she glided toward my table, I realized Jasmine's

almond eyes, creamy skin, and short black hair resembled Jennifer Jones in *Love Is a Many Splendored Thing*. Every guy in the bistro watched her slight, sexy body wiggle toward my table. She ordered us two Bacardis. I'd seen actors drink them in the movies, and I wanted her to think I was cool, too.

"So you're married to a Hungarian...I've never married, of course I've had opportunities...the problem is I always get hung up on married men. I'm a legal secretary. Right now I'm seeing the stockbroker next door. His wife's a bitch. No future, but what a hunk!" She stuck out her chest and posed for the discreetly staring men in the room. "Oh, married men...I don't know why I keep doing it. But there are so few attractive guys in San Francisco."

I tried to take it all in while gulping my Bacardi, hoping Jasmine wouldn't think I was a square.

***

A week later, Jasmine picked me up at our apartment before class. "Jasmine, I'd like you to meet my husband, Anton Denson."

She smiled seductively. Anton's brow wrinkled. "Nice to meet you, may I offer you a drink, maybe a Coke before class?"

"No thanks," she struck a pose, "we're kind of late. Maybe another time."

"Perhaps you and your husband would like to join us for dinner one evening," Anton suggested.

"I don't have a husband," she threw out her chest. "I do have a boyfriend, but his wife probably wouldn't let him come." She winked at Anton. He looked at her like she was one of the hippies.

That night in bed, Anton was vexed. "What are you doing keeping company with that woman? ...*Gutin himmel*, Joanie, where do you find such people?"

***

Jasmine thought Anton a disappointment. Her blatant contempt offended me, and I listed his many admirable qualities. "He's a good man, and I don't appreciate your running him down."

"Why are you with a foreigner? He's so serious, don't you want some romance in your marriage?"

I'm defective, if you want to know the truth, incapable of romance with a man. But I'd never be able to tell her the truth. "Listen, Jasmine, the bloom was never on the rose in the first place, so let's just drop it, okay?

"Joan, you're only 30 years old. You could still get someone exciting and rich, you know? Reach for the stars, Joan, take some risks!"

Finally, someone was responding to my silent frustration. She really got to me. Anton was holding me back; no wonder I was empty. Why not blame him for everything wrong with my life?

At Angie's after class, Jasmine summed up my situation. She seemed to be quoting from the pages of *Sex and the Single Girl.* "What you need is a romantic new beginning. I can see you're bored. It's not fair to you or Anton. I can show you the life you've been missing." Her eyebrows raised mischievously, Jasmine could've been the devil, or she could've been my last chance. She suggested I consult with her attorney boss regarding the irreconcilable differences in our marriage.

Anton was oblivious to my change in attitude. It wasn't his fault, rather my well-honed ability to deceive. He believed we had an ideal life and a perfect marriage; we never quarreled, he acquiesced to most of my requests, and I had freedom to attend school or see girlfriends in the evenings while he watched TV until he fell asleep.

One evening after dinner, I took a deep breath and blurted out, "Anton, I'm not happy, I want a separation."

He was stunned. "It's that Jasmine," he shouted. His face grew red. "I knew she was trouble. You're an innocent. I've met women like her in Hungary. They are witches! The first time I saw her I recognized her for what she is. She's like the gypsies in Budapest. 'Hold on to what you have' my papa always said, 'gypsies steal everything.' Joan, you have no experience in life. You are making a big mistake, but you will be back, you will see. She's big trouble. I know things."

He assumed I'd come under the influence of a free-living woman who hated him. He was pretty accurate.

It was a week before I summoned the guts to move out. Jasmine took charge, arranging for an ultra-modern, furnished apartment in a singles' high-rise near the Golden Gate Bridge.

"Remember to take off your shoes before you come in," said Jasmine curtly, while removing her slingbacks in the foyer of our swanky new pad. "You don't want to track dirt on the white shag carpet." Shoes off at the door was exactly how we'd lived at my mother's house. *But Chicago streets were always muddy. What's Jasmine's problem?* I half expected plastic covers on the couches.

The spectacular harbor view almost made up for the black-and-white decor, but not quite. Where the hell had she found black-and-white plastic roses?

Interior design wasn't the only area in which we disagreed. Attracting men wasn't the problem; they were available. But available for what? Dinner and a goodnight kiss at the door? Hardly. Without putting out there might be a second date, never a third.

The new sexual attitudes terrified me. This wasn't college. I'd stumbled into the era of free love. We joined all the chic young professional groups. Jasmine enjoyed guiding me through the desperate world of swinging singles, predatory in her low-cut dresses and blase sophistication. I didn't know what to think: Chicago ladies didn't wear decolletage!

One Friday night, Jasmine dragged me to a meeting of the "Nob Hill Notables." The smoky room was packed with upwardly mobile singles on the prowl. I perched awkwardly on a bar stool. A tall man in a three-piece suit and receding hairline slid next to me and struck up a conversation.

"Hi, Jon Goldsmith." He rested his arms on the bar, exposing gaudy gold cuff links. "And you are…"

"Joan."

"All right," he leaned closer, "ever hear of the commodities exchange?" He raised his whiskey glass. I smiled stiffly. "Yes, ole Jon's got a seat. Cost me a bundle. I'm divorced, 42, no kids. How old are you?"

"Thirty." *What am I doing here? I left my safe sweet husband to meet men like this?*

"I'll bet you're divorced, no kids. We're a perfect pair. I love your black suit, Joan, those sloppy hippie chicks turn me off. How about dinner tomorrow night? Come on, Ondine's in Sausalito." He dangled it in front of me like a carrot, and I bit.

I'd heard Ondine's was a hip celebrity hangout. Maybe I'd see Warren Beatty. I needed some kind of shot in the arm. I was bored to tears with my new exciting life. "Sure, cool."

***

The maitre d' escorted us to the window table Jon reserved, "How about that view, baby?" He'd probably forgotten my name. He barked at the waiter, "We'll have a bottle of your best Mum's, you like champagne?" I nodded. He didn't notice. "Brut, very brut," he pointed at the waiter. "Your old Jon's a real brute of a guy." He chuckled. I didn't get the joke, but smiled anyway. I searched the tables for celebrities.

After dinner, Jon drove out to the Marina District. Suddenly we turned a sharp corner into the driveway of his split-level home. He pressed a button, and the garage swallowed us up in one gulp, the door must have been greased with Vaseline. I refused to get out.

Jon rattled on about finally finding a nice respectable girl to take home to his mother, and without skipping a beat took my hand and put it on his crotch. I jumped and yanked it back. It was too much for him.

"Oh, shit, baby, you sure have hang-ups!" He slammed the steering wheel. I though he'd smash the Continental into a wall, as we roared backward before the door was halfway up. Mercifully, we sped in silence toward my home.

I leaned against the elevator button and put my head back

against the wall, waiting an eternity for the doors to open and take me away from the humiliating, bizarre evening. I didn't know whether to laugh or cry, and wondered what had happened to the respect that men used to show women. Free love was simple: Guys scored for free. Buying a prostitute was more expensive than buying someone dinner in exchange for sleeping together. Audrey Hepburn wouldn't have permitted anyone to treat her with such disregard. The world's gone crazy.

Where's Rosemary Clooney, while Janis Joplin screams profanity from the rooftops? Does anyone even understand what Bob Dylan's saying? I stomped across the white shag carpet, shoes and all. *Make dirt, not war!*

I hadn't heard from Anton since the separation. Maybe he'd met a new girl. He could be in love with some blonde by now. He could be filing for divorce. My head was starting to ache from the dinner wine wearing off, and the pangs of regret for what I'd done to Anton. How could I have listened to Jasmine's nonsense about finding Mr. Right. There was no such man. Jasmine had turned out to be a scavenger. She dated the men I rejected.

After that night, I became more panicked with each passing day. I finally worked up the courage to make the call. Anton's foreign accent had never sounded so good.

"Well, it's nice to hear your voice, Joan. It has been a while. Matter of fact, I vas planning to call you this week. I've been offered a big promotion in Los Angeles."

"Congratulations, Mr. Executive," I oozed. "What do you say we discuss this over dinner? I'd like to take you out to your birthday next Saturday."

Anton's birthday was going to be my opportunity for an evening of contrite confession to the crime of falling under Jasmine's spell. Only my sexiest dress, the much too tight yellow number, would do for this mission.

Anton's hazel eyes widened as he stood to greet me at the table. I floated into his outstretched arms, "You look terrific, Anton. What's that wonderful aftershave?"

He frowned and looked away. "It is Imperial. You gave it to me for my birthday last year."

"Yes, of course," I stammered. I was petrified. His cold stare scared me. "Anton, I've made a terrible mistake. I've missed you, and I know I hurt you badly. What can I do to make it up to you?"

"Calm down, Joanie." He reached for my hand. "What's important is you came to your senses. I knew she was troublemaker. Such people do not rest until they bring everyone down." I relaxed. He would take me back. "You went looking for excitement and were too trusting, honey. You have lived sheltered life. It is behind us."

Darling Anton, you'll never know how unsheltered my life has been, I thought to myself. It was wonderful to hear we would be reconciling while house hunting in Beverly Hills.

***

I needed to break the news to Jasmine right away. My legs were weak as the elevator jerked to a halt at the 15th floor. She was ironing a blouse in the dining room.

"Jasmine, I have some big news."

She glanced up indifferently. "Yes, what? You're getting married?"

"Anton and I are moving to Los Angeles next month."

That got her attention. She stood the iron up on its end. "What about your half of the rent?"

"You'll get the money, Jasmine." I said, with no regrets.

Tinseltown Hippie

I n Beverly Hills, my whole life changed. Our home looked like it had been plunged into a fondue pot of green goddess dressing. The olive velvet sofa matched the shag carpet and fake tree. The kitchen appliances stood on the counter, an army of avocado soldiers.

What Beverly Hills lacked in San Franciscan charm it made up for with glamour. One evening, I ran out for a carton of milk and rolled my cart over a large pair of shoes. "Excuse me!"

"Don't mention it, honey. You drunk driving?" It was Jack Nicholson, flashing that famous little-boy grin. I didn't ask for an autograph. Angelinos were too cool for that.

***

Late one afternoon, about a month after we'd arrived, Anton brought me to meet one of his oldest friends. He climbed into our new white Mercury sedan, excited. "I can't wait for you to meet Marcus," he beamed, "he's the most successful garment manufacturer in Beverly Hills, and the envy of everyone on our street in Budapest. You won't believe his house!"

"I'm sure it's wonderful, honey." A house was a house to me. Or so I thought.

"Marcus was always smart. When I came to this country, he said 'Anton, get yourself into an Ivy league school and marry a beautiful sorority girl.'"

Even the breeze felt rich, as we drove up Roxbury Drive under a cathedral-like arch of trees. Just beyond Sunset Boulevard, Anton stopped the car. My mouth fell open.

We were parked in front of the biggest mansion I'd ever seen in my life.

"Was I lying?" Anton laughed as we pulled up to a wrought-iron gate. After he shouted our names into a speaker, we eased around the circular driveway to the door.

As he reached for the brass knocker, the door swung open and a maid greeted us with, "Ola. La familia esta aqui." We followed her through an entry hall that could have been an MGM set of the Southwest, complete with fake cacti, serapes, Indian clay pots and Mexican paintings by Tamyo and Ruffino. Green goddess had taken over Roxbury Drive, too. There was an enormous piano in the center of the room, over which hung an enormous olive-green silk tapestry.

A swarthy, large man with a mustache sat on the burnt-orange sofa, drink in hand. A small attractive woman sat next to him with an arm around their son. The child was in tennis shorts.

The man leaped to his feet and stood over us like a tower. "Anton, my long lost friend!" Anton was hidden in his bear hug.

He turned to me and kissed my hand. "Your wife, what's her name, again?"

I smiled my phony demure smile, "I'm Joan."

He searched my face. "Where do you find a Joan in the Old Testament?"

Anton jumped in. "She was named for her father's mother, Jacoba."

Marcus didn't hold anything back. I wasn't surprised he'd done well. I wondered whether he'd fought for Hungarian independence as Anton had. He didn't seem the type.

Marcus pointed at the couch. "And here's my wife, beautiful Bernice." Her shy nervous smile never left the high-gloss floor. "This is our pride and joy, Nathan."

Nathan dutifully shook hands and announced he had a lesson, grabbing his tennis racket and disappearing into the cavernous front hall.

At dinner, the four of us sat at a banquet table made for 20. While Anton and Marcus talked about business, I turned to Bernice.

"I understand you father is a cardiologist; are you in medicine, too?"

"No, I never liked school. My father insisted I attend Stanford, but I married Marcus the first semester and got pregnant right away. I like being a housewife, actually."

As the maid heaped seafood, chicken and paella on our plates, Anton fairly swooned. "I never tasted anything so good!"

A silver tureen was next. It contained a spongy-looking mound swimming in dark liquid.

"Wait until you taste this," boasted Marcus, "it's called flan." He passed it around for us to inspect. "Egg pudding, not like the kugels our mamas made in old country," he smirked, "egg pudding with caramel sauce. Very elegant."

"Delicious." Anton applauded the dessert.

At the end of the evening, we gathered in the doorway exchanging compliments and saying goodbye. Marcus stood under the yellow lamp at the entrance and shot me a wink. The muted light accentuated the dark circles under his eyes and as the wink grew, it became a leer.

Marcus gradually drew us into his fold of wealthy Hungarian friends. It was an extensive, important network of men. Next to each physician, entrepreneur and attorney sat a childlike wife, glassy-eyed with either contentment or boredom, I wasn't sure which.

The mansion was the hub of all their power, a mighty steamship with Marcus at the helm. I wondered what happened to anyone who wanted off.

***

Meanwhile, I was becoming a new woman. But what kind? Should I take riding lessons like Jackie Kennedy or do charity work like the other wives? Nah, they did it to make connections for their husbands, and Anton didn't need me for that.

My husband had become the new meteor in a firm that served the investment needs of its celebrity clients. He'd taken on the attitude and polish of a star. No longer the young guerrilla fighter with the heavy accent and tortured soul, I missed my vulnerable friend.

And what had I become? A Beverly Hills matron. I'd hired a uniformed maid to serve at my fancy dinner parties, which I ran like a drill sergeant. I saw them as necessary social evils, to be overcome with speed and skill.

One evening I was so nervous that I didn't notice the couple still eating their dinner. I directed the maid to "clear everything," and as his roast beef slipped away, the bewildered husband clutched his plate in one hand and speared a chunk of meat with the other.

His impish wife, Judy, cheered him on. "Go for it, Art! Don't give in! It's yours!" Her laughter filled the room, and I breathed for the first time that night.

I'd liked Judy from the start. I'd met her at a charity auxiliary meeting in Beverly Hills. The women were engaging in an annoying process of introducing themselves by name and husband's occupation. Judy stood up and announced, "I'm Judith Sanders, and my husband's a pimp." The stunned silence was broken when Judy amended her statement, "Okay, I'm a French teacher, and my husband's a physician." It had been my first good laugh in too long.

When the meeting ended, I caught her trying to sneak away. I was dying to meet her. When I asked her if she'd be back, she vowed, "this is my first and last auxiliary meeting."

"Well, then, you'll have to give me your phone number, because you just gave me the best laugh I've had in years."

***

As we sifted through the sale rack at Joseph Magnin, Judy tossed her dark head in my direction, disgusted, "This is all such junk, don't you think?"

"Yes. Enough shopping, let's have lunch. I'm starving." I was pushing her three-year-old, Jamie, in his stroller.

Over lunch, Judy sighed, "I feel guilty charging all this stuff. Art's only been practicing six months, and I'm spending money he hasn't brought home yet. I really miss teaching."

"Why stop?"

"Oh, my mom thinks mothers belong at home with their small children. Maybe she's right."

"*C'est dommage, mon ami!* I guess you have to be the perfect mother for a while. When he's in school, you can resume your life as a wild woman!"

"*Quelle savoir-faire!*"

"*Je suis perdu*, and that is my entire French repertoire, Madame."

"Your accent is great."

"You should hear my Hungarian, " Good God, Joanie, when vill you be a sensible vife?"

Bits of salad flew from her mouth, "Joan, you're awful, I love it!"

I glanced at a poster for a concert that weekend. "Does Oscar Levant interest you at all?"

"I've memorized every word he's ever written. Let's go."

It was good to hear someone else was bored with the lifestyle that was supposed to make women so happy. I finally had a soul mate. Perhaps I might someday tell this friend my secret.

***

A handsome young waiter, probably an actor by day, poured champagne into my outstretched glass. I snatched a canapé from a passing silver tray and stepped into the living room. I nearly dropped everything when Marcus grabbed me from behind and grunted in my ear, "Well, Joan, are you ready for the big moment?"

Marcus unhooked himself from me and pointed a remote at the television. "Everyone come close, they're about to drop the ball in Times Square!"

Guy Lombardo flickered into view as guests from all over the house gathered in the living room. Everyone wore unnaturally bright faces as if this New Year's Eve was their greatest night ever.

I had to get away. I wandered through the labyrinthine hallways, stopping at Nathan's door. He sat in the midst of an enormous train set. Whistling metal cars moved back and forth through mountains and over bridges. A freight train belched miniature puffs of smoke.

"You can come in, Mrs. Denson," he waved me inside. "Do you like electric trains?"

"Yes, they're great. My dad gave me a train set when I was just about your age." I could feel my father next to me, as we followed the train through its small towns. I looked at Nathan through misty eyes. I longed to hold the curly-haired child in my arms.

"So, here you hide, Joan, with your new boyfriend, you missed the ball dropping." Marcus had slipped in quietly.

Nathan was embarrassed by Marcus's "funny" remark and had immediately stopped his friendly chatter. Marcus could be so insensitive. If Nathan were my son, I'd never embarrass him.

"Where have you been?" Anton was annoyed and disappointed, I'd missed our kiss. He handed me a glass of champagne. I pecked him on the cheek and drank the glass in one gulp. Then I asked for another, and another and another, but my longing for a child of my own wouldn't be squelched.

***

I staggered into the living room of our apartment, leaning on Anton, as he said, "I've never seen you like this. You are absolutely drunk."

"Oh, you're just an old prude. It's New Year's Eve, everyone gets drunk."

"This is not the Joanie I've known since she was 22."

"This Joanie wants a child! Anton I want us to have a baby. I'm almost 31. Everyone else has a baby to love!"

"But you have me." He attempted a hug. I backed away.

"Talk lower. You're drunk, and you're getting loud."

"Let them hear! Who cares!"

"All right, that's it. You need to sleep."

He tried to pull me into the bedroom. I yanked my arm away.

"And the doctor asked us *only* to do it in the week my temperature rises, but not you, the big war hero. No temperature charts for you! All you care about is your stupid desire. Your stupid desire and that's all!" If the neighbors were listening, they might as well hear the good stuff.

I grabbed the fake olive tree and hurled it in his direction. It crashed through the glass coffee table a few feet away. Horrified, Anton rushed around shutting windows. I followed behind him shrieking.

"You're killing me. I hate your guts!"

The doorbell rang. Anton opened it to reveal two police officers. "I'm sorry, Mr. Denson, your neighbor said she heard bloodcurdling screams. Is everything all right?"

"Well, my wife got drunk for the first time in her life. She's making a scene over nothing."

"Nothing, you call having a baby nothing? I pounded his chest. One policeman stifled a smile, while the other picked me up and carried me to the bedroom.

"You need to sleep this off. Can you get undressed by yourself?"

I started to sob. "I don't want to go to bed. I don't want to get undressed." I just couldn't stop crying. He whispered to Anton, and in seconds they had my dress off and my nightgown slipped over my head.

As Anton approached to pick me up, I socked him. Hard.

He left the room, and the policemen convinced me to lie down. They gently pulled the blankets up to my chin. I mumbled, "I want a baby and nobody cares."

"You'll feel better in the morning, Mrs. Denson. Please lay off the booze."

I started to fade while they stood in the hall with Anton, talking in low voices.

***

Nine months later we were blessed with a son. I sat alone, cradling Jerry on my lap while he sucked his bottle. I stroked his perfectly shaped head, so much like his father's. His feedings were the most serene moments of my life.

Now I have it all: a beautiful baby, a devoted husband, and good friends.

***

The telephone jolted me out of sleep.

"Oh, hi Glenda, why are you up so early?"

"I've been on the phone for hours. Myrna called at 7 am, that bitch, to say she'll be out of town all next month. Bridge will be cancelled unless we can find a fourth. Do you know anyone?"

"I'll ask Lois. She's the captain of the bowling team."

"Do you use the lawn or go into one of those stinky alleys?"

"It's for a good cause. We'll talk later."

The next afternoon I caught Lois in the locker room. "One of our bridge girls is out of town. Do you know anyone who plays? They don't have to be good." Lois, due to an insatiable thirst for gossip, knew everyone.

Actually, I do know one girl, Vicky Berck. But I must warn you, she's very strange. She's not your type, a sort of hippie who reads all the time. Nobody can figure out why she divorced a fabulous guy. Her parents are wealthy, and they've given up on her. She does play bridge and probably could fill in."

*A hippie who reads all the time would certainly be an improvement over this stupid bowling....*I took her number.

"Hi, is this Vicky?"

"Yes." She seemed surprised, as if she didn't get many calls out of the blue.

"I'm Joan Denson. Lois Malone gave me your number. My friends and I play bridge once a week, and we wondered if you could fill in for a month."

"I haven't played in a while. Is it a cutthroat game?" She sounded nervous.

"Oh, we never really compete with each other," I lied. "Seven-thirty sharp. See you then."

***

Glenda's doorbell rang at 7:30. I opened the door. "Hi, I'm Joan, you must be Vicky."

Before me stood the perfect California girl: slim, tan and blonde. Her eyes took me in completely. She smiled. I tingled inside. Long, straight hair framed her face and pink granny glasses. *So what, other women smile at you. Relax.*

She reminded me of Cindy's clean-cut good looks. There was something about her pseudo hippie outfit. I'd spotted that fringed suede jacket at Saks the previous week. She had chutzpah, she was a little daring—she was maybe more than a little daring.

She glanced at me for a second and turned her head away. I returned to the bridge table and made introductions, watching her cross the room.

Halfway through the game, I noticed Vicky growing frustrated. She slumped over her cards, elbows on the table, staring at her hand despondently.

I immediately made a foolish blunder on purpose. Across the table, my bridge partner's eyes turned to stone. I looked at Vicky, who sat with her mouth agape. Then she started to giggle, and bit her lip. Our wordless conversation began.

An hour later we stood by the kitchen counter laughing and drinking Cokes. "It's hard for me to believe you're as bad a bridge player as I am," she looked me in the eye.

"I'm quite famous for my incompetence," I winked. She hadn't been fooled.

"You know, the stage is your calling, Joan. You're a good actress, but not good enough."

"I bet you can't wait to be my partner, huh?"

"Not if you trump my ace," she smiled shyly.

The next morning, I sprang to the phone.

"Hi."

"Hi, yourself," Vicky answered.

"Am I calling too early?"

"No, my dad expects me at the office: I work Saturdays. It's a bummer."

"So when we said goodnight after the game, we were talking about Chekhov. I never met anyone who liked that stuff."

"Yes," her voice was soft. For a moment, neither of us spoke. I sensed her anxiety but didn't want to let her go.

"Hey, there's a great old '30s movie, *Forty-Second Street...*"

"...with Ruby Keeler..."

"It's playing next Saturday."

"Great, we'll do it. I really have to get moving, work..."

"Okay, bye." My heart raced.

***

The following Saturday I sped to Vicky's apartment. Though a half-hour early, I didn't want to appear anxious so I parked and arranged my hair and makeup. *This is ridiculous, you can't sit here forever.* I walked slowly up to her building, held my breath, lifted the receiver and rang the intercom. "Hi, it's Joanie."

"Great, I'll buzz you in."

As soon as she opened the door, I feared I'd made a huge mistake.

While she was on the phone, I listened to her sudden bursts of laughter and watched her pace as she spoke. Her intensity made her seem reckless. There we were, just the two of us, no friends to act as a buffer between her personality and mine. *Maybe I should just make an excuse and leave while she's on the phone. Every move she makes is so impulsive. She could be trouble.*

"Sorry, that was my mom." She walked me to the bookcase. "Joan, meet my best friends."

Her library spanned the entire living room wall. Chekhov, Gogol, Dostoevsky, English philosophers, Italian playwrights, and Spanish poets. She was too good to be true. I pulled out a book.

"No, no," she chuckled, "we're late."

***

The old Nuart Theater was deserted.

"It's just us and the ghosts of Christmas past." Vicky eased herself into a frayed velvet seat. We shared popcorn and Raisinettes, tapping our feet to the pulsating rhythm of Ruby's dancing feet. Vicky's citrus scent filled me with pleasure each time she brushed against me."

Sunlight blinded us as we emerged from the theater on Santa Monica Boulevard. She turned to me, "Hey, it's still early. My favorite hangout's nearby."

I stiffened. She noticed.

"Relax, it's not a bar."

Books lined the floor-to-ceiling shelves in every direction. Sweet incense mixed with the musty odor of aged paper. We sat together on a ragged sofa in Papa Bach's used bookstore, watching people climb little stepladders to reach their treasure.

"I've spent a lot of time here since my divorce. Don't you love the old Tiffany lamps? There's a kind of comfort here, do you feel it?"

I stared into her eyes. "Yes, I feel it."

***

A few weeks later, she phoned. "Would you like to have dinner downtown? *The Cherry Orchard* is at the Chandler Pavilion.

"Yes, providing you do pickup and delivery. Anton wouldn't want me driving downtown at night."

There was a slight edge to her voice. "Tell him I'm a good driver."

"Okay, okay. I have to go. I need to make dinner."

That Wednesday, I stood on the curb, nervously watching Vicky fly up the street in her fire-engine red *Spider*, golden hair exploding in every direction. She roared to a stop in front of me. "Sharp car. Do you think you could put up the top?"

"I figured you'd ask. God forbid we mess up the hairdo."

"I'm not getting in until you put up the top, Vicky!"

"Joanie, your hairspray is as good as a helmet. We could turn over and you'd survive." I couldn't help but laugh. "There's a scarf and a sweater in the backseat. Come on, let's go."

"I'm not getting in until you put up the top." I turned away to intimidate her.

"Let's not waste a beautiful summer night." She got out and took my hands. She smelled like fresh limes. "Come on, it'll be fun." She slipped behind the wheel and pushed open my door. The moment I dropped into the bucket seat, the car lurched forward and we were off.

That Fiat hung so low to the ground I could feel the white line down the middle of the road. Vicky took corners at top speed, weaving through traffic. We got on the 405 freeway.

"You're not on the open road. This city has a speed limit!"

"Thanks for the driving tips, Joanie, but this city also has a theater, and we're late!"

My fear seemed to inspire her to break the sound barrier. The scarf blew off, releasing my lacquered hair to the wind. I felt a rush of joy—an exhilarating freedom. I thought of Cindy's kisses.

***

We began to see each other regularly. We called each other almost every day. I began to realize a scary truth. Vicky filled my soul. Anton couldn't do this. My love for my baby was completely different, too.

Jerry was only 11 months old. It felt wrong to leave him in the evenings without someone proper to take care of him. A live-in housekeeper would be my passport to freedom. When Anton became a junior partner, I presented my case.

"A housekeeper? For what? My mother did all the work, and she had five children."

I bristled. "Your mother isn't here to do the work. I'm sure all the successful families in Hungary had housekeepers."

I'd appealed to his tiny streak of snobbery. The live-in

housekeeper relieved my guilt and left me free to see Vicky. As a dutiful wife and mother, I made certain Anton and Jerry were fed before I left home in the evenings. Anton would utter a sigh and relax into his easy chair. The sigh was my escape signal. He would soon be asleep.

His expectations of me had been limited but specific. He wanted his wife to be intelligent, pretty and charming. But with my increased absence, he seemed to be more possessive. Was it him, or had I begun to resent giving him any time that could be spent with Vicky?

With Jerry tucked in, I sped to Vicky's door. Mondays and Wednesdays were movie nights, and Fridays were bridge. Seated in the dark theater, elbows sharing an armrest, our fever mounted. But we never touched, and we never talked about what was happening.

Eight months after our first meeting, she called me unexpectedly. She sounded strange. Had I done something to offend her?

"Joanie, can you meet me at my apartment tonight? We need to talk."

Rigid, in her red-velvet armchair, Vicky appeared composed despite the slight quiver in her voice.

" I find I can't see you anymore, and I really can't tell you why. I'm sorry." She looked away.

We sat in silence. I began to sob. She didn't offer any words, any comforting hand. I got up and walked out.

On the drive home, I felt profound despair, mixed with relief. I'd never see her again, but at least I'd been sensible this time. The stakes were higher this time. I had a baby to protect, and I was playing it safe.

9 Oblivion

The moment I returned home I rushed to the baby's room and rocked him in my arms. Nothing and no one would wrench him from me.

In bed next to Anton, I wrapped my arms around his sleeping body. Acting normal would keep me safe. Everything would be fine now that Vicky was gone. She'd done me a favor.

I admired the sheen of Anton's black wavy hair against the white pillowcase. He was so handsome. I enjoyed watching women flirt with him. I knew they didn't have a chance; he would never stray.

I'd overheard his friends once at a poker game. When they bragged about conquests at the office, Anton piped up, "When you have the best, why try the rest?" It shut them right up. After all I'd put him through, he still loved and admired me, and I wasn't going to forget how lucky I was to have him.

Yet while I had preserved tranquility in my daily life, my dreams began to plague me. I was back at Harcourt and facing Dean Potts and charges of immoral conduct. This time I was convicted and expelled, only it was with Vicky. In the worst of the nightmares, Vicky and I would walk down the dorm corridor holding suitcases, while girls on either side jeered and spit in our face. I woke up screaming.

"Joanie! Wake up, you were having bad dream."

"I saw us get killed in a car crash!" One lie so easily led to another.

"Darling, I tell you, never watch late news. You saw a crash story last night."

"Yes, you're right, Anton. I'm sorry for waking you. No

more late news." We lay back down. I felt the warmth of his backside solidly against me. In was good to be his wife.

Still, I couldn't get Vicky out of my mind. We had only been friends, and over the years I'd had many close girl-friends and hadn't become a prisoner of those experiences. What was different about Vicky? Why did I melt at the thought of her? The intense way she'd look at me Her shy vulnerability and adorable smile. She was a paradox of sophisti-cated innocence that had me by the heart.

I knew she'd been seeing a therapist. There was no doubt he'd encouraged her to back away from a potentially danger-ous situation. Should I make a move? Maybe just call and say hello...

Don't be stupid, she'll take it as a sexual invitation. That's ridiculous. You have no way of knowing what she thinks.

Another, more frustrating, dream developed where Vicky kept phoning, but I couldn't reach the receiver. I'd wake up sweaty and grab the receiver, only to hear an empty dial tone.

Every day I fought the impulse to call her. *Anton will find out, and he will take away the baby, is that what you want?...You'll face another trial, this time as an unfit mother. You're jeopardizing your life for a fling...I don't want a fling...I want to live with her, to be a family with her. Impossible. You need help, maybe Dr. Marx. Vicky rejected you anyway. Anyone who'd blow you off like that is no better than Cindy.*

Four months passed. It was September of 1971, and we were celebrating the Jewish New Year. I sent her a greeting card with a simple inscription: "I hope you're doing well. Happy New Year. Warm Regards, Joanie."

I stood at the post office, my hand poised above the mail slot. *This is just a friendly card. Oh, quit kidding yourself, you love her. But if I mail this card, my whole life would change. It'll be a lot harder and scarier.* I released the card and watched it slide through into darkness.

A second later I panicked, and tried to force my hand inside the shoot. *Where's that damn card?* I looked around and tried to compose myself. The only other person there, an older man, pretended not to see the crazy woman with her hand in the slot. I could barely touch the tip of the envelope. *Damn!* It was no use.

Just as expected, I got the call.

"Hi, Joanie, it was so nice hearing from you. I've missed you."

"I've missed your company, too." My words sounded stilted and insincere. I took a deep breath, shifting my weight from foot to foot, trying to be casual. "You're my only friend whose even heard of Ruby Keeler." Now I sounded stupid. My mind went blank.

"Is that why you contacted me, Joanie?" You need a buddy who likes old movies?

"No, not really." Another deep breath..."I've missed you."

"How about dinner Wednesday at our usual place?"

"I'll be there at 7."

***

The steak house on Wilshire was crowded when I arrived. I could see her from the street, sitting at a table near the window. When she waved at me, I could feel beads of perspiration between my breasts. I wanted to run away. I wanted to kiss her all over. We greeted each other with an awkward handshake.

Nothing had changed. The restaurant lighting illuminated her honey-blonde hair and creamy complexion. *A shiksa goddess.* Except she wasn't a shiksa; she was something much more forbidden.

She handed me a tiny box wrapped in gold paper with a fringed bow. My fingers tingled as I opened the black-velvet case—a gold Star of David.

"It's gorgeous" I don't have a Star of David!" *Why am I always tongue tied around her?*

"It's a Spanish antique, from the 14th century. I knew it would look beautiful on you."

We avoided talking about what had gone on before. She knew my card signified that I was there for more than friendship, just as her gift meant the same.

The next Friday, Vicky threw a party. She invited Judy and Glenda from the bridge group and some of her old friends. For some reason, she declared emphatically that she would not be inviting one friend in particular because, "She's too uptight!" I didn't really know what she meant, but it was her party.

After an extravagant buffet dinner, eight of us sat around her living room table talking. My friend Judy sat alongside Glenda, who held court with outrageous stories of romances she'd had as a New York society chanteuse. Vicky brought out a tray of chocolate cake and strange-looking cigarettes, which I recognized from my Haight-Ashbury interviews.

Everyone, but me, screeched with delight. Vicky lit a joint, inhaled deeply and passed it over. I inhaled and coughed convulsively, pushing it away to Glenda. After a while, the guests, my straitlaced friend Judy included, started to giggle foolishly. They began devouring mounds of chocolate cake with their hands.

Idiots, I thought. I never believed Judy and Glenda were like that. I behaved more appropriately than they, me with the worst secret.

At midnight, the party started to break up.

"Joanie, would you mind driving me home? I'm still pretty dizzy." Glenda was whirling around the room, her perfectly arranged platinum hair disheveled. The residue of her bright-red lipstick smudged across her face in tawdry streaks.

"Sure, I better take Judy, too."

"No, it's still early!" Judy had exchanged her navy blazer for a Grateful Dead T-shirt borrowed from Vicky's closet. We managed to talk her into leaving, but she would not surrender the shirt. At the door, Vicky took me aside.

"Joanie, I'm sorry you didn't have a good time. Please say you weren't offended."

"Oh no, you know, smoke hurts my throat." She could see right through me. "Maybe it's more than that." She leaned over me with one hand on the door post. I looked up at her, "I guess I was feeling a little left out. You and everyone else were getting into it, having a good time. I guess I'm too uptight." Her beautiful, even teeth formed a warm smile.

"I'm glad you were here." She patted my arm. "Maybe next time you'll have more fun."

The following Friday night, Vicky invited me over again, alone. She was turning steaks over on a Hibachi when I arrived. Her dining room table was set with the fine china and crystal of a formal matriarch. She never ceased to surprise me, so filled with contradictions.

In the center of the table sat a giant silver salad bowl filled with unfamiliar vegetables. She served me a large portion of salad to start. "Eat hearty, it's good for you." She sat opposite me, grinning.

"What are those little brown twigs?"

"Oh, they're herbs, Dim sum herbs from the farthest corners of China."

"They're edible?"

"Yes, very." Again, that stupid grin.

As we ate, the pictures on the wall started to become distorted, and I developed an insatiable thirst. Red wine trickled down my throat like fruit punch. Eventually Vicky took the bottle away, firmly.

"Joanie, you've had enough."

I dove into the chocolate cake with the same fervor as her guests a week earlier. I started to giggle, "This was the best dinner, and I want the recipe for the salad. I'm going to call Judy right now and tell her how much fun I'm having!"

"You're in no shape, sit down and take some deep breaths."

"You're just like Anton; you don't want me to have a fun!"

I was trying to pull away from her and walk to the balcony when the nausea hit. I ran to the bathroom and gripped the toilet bowl, trying to speak between gasps, "I don't...know...why I'm so sick." All I could do was hold on. *Maybe I'll die and fall in.*

"Let me hold your head," Vicky steadied me from behind.

"Don't touch me! I have to take off my hair!"

"Your hair?"

I ripped the shoulder-length fall that I combed into my own long, brunette hair and handed it in a matted ball to Vicky. The vomiting turned to dry heaves.

"You can't go home tonight, Joanie. I can't send you back to Anton wasted like this."

"Maybe the meat was spoiled!"

"No, it wasn't the meat. We'll talk about it tomorrow. Let me get you into these pajamas."

She held me firmly with one hand and undressed me with the other. I covered my face in embarrassment while she undid my padded bra and threw the pretend breasts over a chair. "You know, Joanie, you don't need that ridiculous padded bra. I'm starting to worry that your teeth come out, too!"

I'd never been so embarrassed and so miserable.

"I called Anton; he'll see you in the morning."

"Do I have ptomaine poisoning?"

"No, you'll feel better if you sleep. We'll see how things go tomorrow. I'll be on the couch."

"No, I don't like to sleep alone. I just want to go home now."

"Joanie, it's a twin bed, there isn't room for both of us."

But I wouldn't relent. Neither of us slept much. She didn't touch me except to apply cold compresses to my forehead. I was in and out of the bathroom all night. I'd wake up sweating and confused. The night seemed to last forever. Finally, I awoke to the smell of freshly brewed coffee and a terry cloth robe across the foot of the bed. I wandered out to the kitchen.

"You know, I feel fine now. What could have made me so sick?"

"Joanie, you're going to kill me. You have the right to kill me. I…"

Silence.

"What?"

"I spiked the salad with marijuana."

"What? You did what?" I grabbed the coffee pot and cocked my arm back, I didn't know what I was doing, but I was furious.

She grabbed the pot out of my hand and laid it safely on the counter behind her. "Look, there were just a few twigs of marijuana in the salad. I wanted to lighten things up. Just give you a little buzz."

"A what?" She stared at the floor. "You damned well poisoned me!"

"I know, I know." She couldn't look at me, "It's just that, at school we'd do it all the time. Cake…brownies…but no one ever got sick like that. Please forgive me."

"I didn't know if I can." Her eyes filled with tears as I grabbed my coat and left.

***

A week had gone by and no call. Had I been too harsh? Or had I cut my losses? Nothing felt right.

Anton was glad to have me around the house in the evenings again. We were eating dinner when the phone rang. Anton picked it up and shot me an angry glance. "Vicky."

"Hi, Vicky, how've you been?" I tried to sound casual, avoiding Anton's icy glare. He wasn't pleased when I'd failed to return home last Friday.

I stretched the cord as far away from Anton as possible while Vicky spilled out as many words of apology as she could fit into my angry silence. "I've been feeling awful about that stupid salad. Would you give me another chance? I've got the menu all planned. Good old, clean-living Campbell's soup. You can't turn that down."

But I should turn it down. I'll be in a compromising situa-

tion again. I know she's dangerous and impulsive. But she makes me feel alive.

"I adore Campbell's soup."

"How about this Friday at 7:30?"

"Fine. See you then."

"And Joanie, leave your padded bra and phony hair with Anton."

I avoided Anton's eyes as I returned to the dinner table, beet red.

"What's wrong with you? You have not been yourself since you got sick at Vicky's house. She's not your kind of person." He sounded more sad than irritated.

My head ached. *Let her go, Joan. Leave her alone.*

"Yes, Anton, maybe she isn't."

***

But the following week, there I was. When she opened the door, I knew it was worth the gamble. I couldn't look away from the outline of her sculpted breasts beneath a tight-fitting sweater. She had opened a bottle of wine. I sipped cautiously from my glass; I wasn't going to fall for any tricks this time.

We shared her red tapestry sofa, listening to a Neil Diamond album. I didn't want an artificial buzz, but I did want to feel her softness.

She ran her fingers through my hair. "It's really yours, right? It's not on loan from Marlo Thomas?" I threw back my head and laughed. She gripped my shoulders, pressed me to her and kissed me deeply. Her confidence thrilled me.

We kissed for two hours, only kissed. But it was enough. I melted, lost in pleasure and excitement. It was nearly 12 before I snapped back to reality and realized I'd better get home.

As I hurried out the door, I called over my shoulder, "Now you can say you made love to a married woman!"

"Joanie. We necked, that's all. Don't feel guilty."

I did feel guilty. What she called "a little necking" was closer to making love than anything I'd experienced in the last

11 years. Was she just playing with me? Was she another Cindy? I put all my hope into the fact that we'd been friends nearly a year before that first kiss.

***

Anton's father died in Budapest shortly after my "necking session" with Vicky. When he flew out to the funeral, I stayed behind with the baby. The following Sunday I phoned Vicky, put Jerry to bed and ordered dinner in.

"Where's the housekeeper?" Vicky wanted to know, peering around the apartment from the doorway.

"She's off 'til Monday night...you like Chicken Delight?"

"My all-time favorite. You're quite a cook."

After dinner, we sat on the sofa listening to a recording of Mike Nichols and Elaine May on Broadway. She laughed at all my favorite parts. We howled at the comedy, that is, until the Elaine May line of the woman about to cheat on her husband, "He trusts me. I wouldn't be doing this if he didn't trust me!"

I looked at Vicky. Her eyes burned like blue coals. No girl had looked at me like that since Cindy. But there was a difference; Vicky was a woman, not a college kid.

She took my hand and led me to the bedroom without a word. Inside, she tenderly stroked my cheek while disrobing me with other, one button at a time. It was warm and dark in the room, the light cast from the living room bathed her face in desire as strong as my own.

She covered my face in butterfly kisses, until at last she reached my mouth and gently opened it with her own.

I went limp as she slithered down the length of my body, spreading her flaxen hair over my exposed skin. It aroused me to a fever pitch. She hesitated, I begged her not to stop, and then she moved to my clitoris. My body shook with torrential spasms. I lay back, flooded with tears of joy.

We spent the entire night making love, each time with a different technique. I couldn't predict her next move. She commanded my body, and I succumbed with abandon.

At one point she stopped, sat up and asked for a Coke.

Feeling rejected, I gaped at her. "Have you lost interest already?"

"No, Joanie," She laughed. "I'm just thirsty, honest."

She meant it. She gulped the entire Coke and came right back to me. We made love until daybreak. I couldn't believe she was real. It was like a reward for so many years spent alone and undiscovered.

We drifted off after dawn, but the cries of the baby startled us from sleep. Vicky threw on her clothes and headed for the door. "I'll grab coffee at work."

I ran to Jerry's room and carried him into the foyer. Vicky stopped at the door, and for a moment, she held my eyes. "Now I can say I've made love to a married woman!"

Sure, she was joking, and yet, I worried. Had I been her "married woman" conquest? That was it. She had me under her thumb, just like that. There I was completely controlled by her after one night. If she wanted, she could just throw me away.

I'm not calling her. I won't get hooked on another Cindy. I can manage without her. Let her call me.

And she did. She phoned the second she arrived at work. I almost cried from painful relief—relief that I mattered, pain that she mattered so deeply.

***

We met every Monday, Wednesday and Friday night in her apartment after that. Movies and discussions were replaced by lovemaking. The absences from her were unbearable.

One night, we lay in her bed silently staring at the voluptuous Toulouse Lautrec ladies on her bedroom walls when a thought crossed my mind. "Have you done this with other girls?"

She smiled. "Actually I had a very intense love affair with a girl named Emily in college. We lived together off campus until my parents started to figure it out. I got sick of hiding it, and I decided to just tell them the truth. Well, they freaked out. They called Emily's parents, who jumped the next plane to California and took her home."

Her face darkened, "There was not one word from Emily after that. Not one letter. Not even a phone call. I felt dead inside. Until I met you."

"But you've been married?"

"My parents were ready to disown me because of Emily. I had to do something. They said I had to either get married or get a job. What could I do for a living? I majored in French and humanities. Girls like me didn't work."

"So you got married to get out of work," I poked her ribs.

"I married my high school sweetheart, Greg. It turned out to be worse than any job I could imagine. Not a day went by that I didn't long for Emily."

"Do you still think about her?" I felt sick. I sounded sympathetic, but wanted to hear that Emily meant nothing.

"I think about her sometimes. I wonder what happened to her. Did she marry some guy? Does she have children? Does she ever think about me?—stupid thoughts."

I wanted to tell her that Emily had probably married, had eight kids and was now obese. But I cared about Vicky's feelings. I didn't want to see her in pain. So I told her what I believed. "I'm sure she missed you terribly. What could she do? She was only a kid."

"She's not a kid anymore, and the phone doesn't ring! Listen, I don't like talking about it. What about you, Joanie? Tell me about your past lovers." She smiled self assuredly, expecting I had no story to tell.

I told her everything: Harcourt, Cindy, the hearing, everything. I'd never breathed a word of the story before, except to Dr. Marx. This secret, that had been my greatest humiliation, actually seemed to gain her respect—at first.

"You know, the worst part was that you got in trouble for next to nothing. A few nights of sex don't make a person's sexual orientation." She had a bias about what she believed was real and what was experimentation. She had her own set of ideas where sex was concerned, and I wondered where they came from. I would find out soon enough.

***

So there I was: a 32-year-old Beverly Hills housewife and mother leading a split life. My mornings at *Mommy and Me* classes ran into Tuesday and Thursday evenings teaching English to immigrants at Fairfax Adult School. I spent Saturday and Sunday nights with Anton and our friends, feigning domestic bliss.

We often doubled with Judy and Art. One night it occurred to me that Vicky and I could never be like this, sitting in a car as a couple. It wasn't fair. I listened distractedly to Judy, "…and I'm due in December. Mother is giving me a fabulous shower next month, put it on your calendar."

So, Judy wouldn't be teaching French again anytime soon. She seemed to forget how much she missed teaching and freedom. I was bursting to talk about Vicky, but I didn't dare tell the truth, even to her. But I needed to talk anyway.

That Saturday, Judy and I headed for the Bullock's tea room, loaded down with packages. After we'd ordered our usual Chinese chicken salads, I looked up at Judy. "I have to tell you something very private, which you must promise never to repeat."

"Sure, what?" She put down her fork and arched her neck, waiting for the news.

"Judy, I'm having an affair."

"You are? Oh, Joanie, you're terrible," she smiled. "What's his name?"

His name? I stared out the window at a restaurant across the street, "Johnny."

"Are you going to divorce Anton for Johnny?" There was a snide tone in her voice and a twinkle in her eyes.

"It's too soon. Uh, Johnny's married too." I had become a natural liar. I wasn't proud of it.

"So you're both married. It's convenient, really. You can just go on having a good time. But Joanie, you should tell

Anton the truth sometime. I know you care about him, and lies always get found out eventually."

It was the last thing I wanted to hear from her. After our talk, Judy pestered me for details all the time. It was harder betraying her than Anton.

In early winter Vicky's mood changed. We had been lovers nearly 10 months, and she seemed distracted, her passion less intense. I started to wonder how she was filling time while I was away.

I decided to ask a few questions the next Monday night we were together. When the time came, I felt a clammy fear— afraid of asking and more afraid of the answers,

I took a deep breath when she came out of the kitchen and joined me on the couch.

"What did you do this weekend, Vicky?"

She flushed. A few seconds passed in silence.

"Well, I saw my parents. Visited friends..." She grinned the way she always did when she danced around the truth.

"Which friends?"

That was it. She got defensive. "Are you saying I'm not allowed to have friends?"

"You're changing the subject!" I was on to her mind tricks. "Why are you being so defensive?"

"You're not my keeper. You're the one who is married, Joan. Remember that!"

"That never seemed to bother you before!" I was about to explode with jealousy. She as much as admitted she was doing whatever she wanted to do with whomever she wanted. She didn't seem to care whether it hurt me or not.

"Look, I need to get home now." I stifled my rage.

"Don't you always 'need to get home,' Joan?" She turned away. "I'll see you on Monday for the usual."

That Sunday I buckled Jerry into his car seat and took off for Brentwood, unannounced.

I pushed her buzzer of her second-floor apartment and watched two frenzied silhouettes behind the drawn drapes of her living room. Even though I suspected it, even though a voice in me had said to get in my car and come here, I still couldn't believe it was really happening. I heard her voice as if it were coming from someone else.

"Who's there?"

"It's Joan and Jerry, thought we'd drop by and say hello."

"Hold on!" Vicky yelled into the intercom.

I wasn't waiting around. But before I could back out the car, a pale, pretty brunette appeared on the sidewalk, looking flushed, as if she'd just emerged from the sack. She leaned into the car and in a lovely British accent asked if I were Vicky's friend, Joanie.

"I'm Sara, an old friend from South Africa. I'm staying here while I get my bearings. Vicky's showering, but she says to come up.

"Tell her thanks, but we were just passing by." I couldn't stand to look at her. Her cheeks bore that rosy glow of good sex.

"Oh what a pity—nice meeting you, hope we'll see you again."

That lousy Saks Fifth Avenue hippie had another girl-friend.

I had two tickets to the Philharmonic in my purse. I slapped them against Vicky's windshield with a note: "I can't make it to this. I know the tickets won't go to waste. Take your South African lover. You're a liar and a fraud, and I never want to see you again."

I drove away enraged, while Jerry slept peacefully through the entire incident.

"Vicky called," Anton looked curious when I came in. "She sounded angry."

"Really?" I felt anxious. Maybe I shouldn't have written the nasty note.

"It's Joan, you wanted to talk to me?" I said in a haughty tone.

"Why did you come here on my day off?"

"Your day off? From me? Am I paying you for your favors?" I whispered so sharply it could've cut glass.

"We have to talk. I'll see you tomorrow night." She hung up abruptly.

Oh, God. Was it over?

I stayed awake most of the night, aching to undo everything from the day. How could she be so faithless? Who was I to expect fidelity? I looked at Anton's sleeping form.

To me, sleeping with another man would be infidelity. But I was sleeping with a woman; I wasn't an adulteress. Whom was I kidding? *Hester Prynne Denson, you are an adulteress.*

On Monday, I arrived at Vicky's place, certain this would be the last time. I was shaking by the time the door opened.

"All right, so you've met Sara. She has more right than you to be here. You know, you have a husband and a family, and I have nothing. You're just using me for sex."

As her eyes overflowed with tears, she looked like a little child crumpled up in a chair.

"That's not true. I'm not using you for sex." *I know what you want, Vicky, and I'm not going to do it. I'm not breaking up my marriage just because my heart is hinged to you.*

"Please be quiet and let me finish." Tiny beads of perspiration collected on the bridge of Vicky's nose. "There's no future for me with you. It's too frustrating to go on like this. Sara's a former lover, she's moving here permanently from Capetown. She's a dentist."

"Congratulations, you'd do anything for a free teeth cleaning."

"Shut up! She's unencumbered, and she wants to live with me. You have a marriage. I want one, too. Maybe mine won't be legal, but it'll be more genuine than yours!"

"Do you love her?"

"I care deeply. No, I don't love her the way I love you...but she's very sweet, and crazy feelings aren't important. You have a marriage. I want a life partner, too."

I stepped forward, our faces inches from one another,

hissing, "Go live with Miss Capetown. I would've divorced Anton to be with you!"

Vicky's mouth dropped open. "You're lying, you'd never do that! You're too spoiled."

"Look who's talking about spoiled, the little princess who works for her daddy is calling me spoiled. I'm willing to give up everything to be with you!

"What would your neighbors say if I moved in?" she shrieked.

"What do I care?" I stood, hands on hips, challenging her, "I'm five minutes' gossip over a cup of coffee, that's all!"

"Bull! You need a husband walking three paces behind you, mink coat in his outstretched arms."

"I hate you. Absolutely hate you with all my heart, Vicky. Get out of my life!"

I slammed the door, and ran down the stairs.

***

We didn't see each other for a month. I thought I saw her everywhere. Is that Vicky's car honking in the street? Is she on the other end of the ringing phone? Is she missing me? Is she making love to Sara? Is she enjoying her more than she enjoyed me?

I drove by her apartment every day, hoping to catch a glimpse of her. Instead of my Tinseltown hippie, I saw Sara coming and going. Vicky didn't see my car, but Miss Capetown sure did.

On one particularly lonely night, I was sitting in the kitchen, disconsolate. *Damn you, Vicky, feel my energy and call.* The sharp ring startled me. I lunged for the receiver. It slipped from my grasp and spiraled to the floor. That was me, dangling—hook, line and sinker.

Oh God, don't hang up! I heard her voice, but I couldn't speak.

"Sara says you drive by everyday. She knows your car."

"I'm so glad you called."

Her voice shook, she lost her cold façade, "I've missed you, too."

"I understand why you want a partner and a life."

"I don't want a generic woman. I just want you."

"I really meant what I said about divorcing Anton."

Her voice grew shrill, "Glenda said you two bought a house in Sherman Oaks!"

"Well, Jerry turned over the Christmas tree here in the lobby. The mirrors are all broken, and the landlord is evicting us. My parents offered to buy us a house. What was I supposed to do?"

"How could you have meant what you said about living with me when you're digging in deeper roots with Anton?"

"I intend to live in that house with you, Vicky. I've been struggling with this since the day I met you. I'm mad about you, I'm terrified of changing my life…but mostly I'm terrified of losing you. That's the truth. And it wouldn't just be me, you know, you'd have to be a parent. That's the end of your freedom."

"Joanie, I wanted to live with you the first moment I saw you. And in case you haven't noticed, I'm more patient with Jerry than you. Remember that day at Denny's when Jerry threw his mashed potatoes all over the place. Who cleaned up and who sat there like a princess?"

We both laughed, exhausted and relieved. "Okay. Just give me some time. I don't want to lose custody. This has to be done carefully. I promise, Vicky, we will be together within the year.

"You'll never get divorced."

"Anton won't stay in the Valley for long. He'll insist we move back, and I'll refuse. He'll go back to the city, and I'll live in the house my parents bought. Trust me, this will work." I listened to the silent line. I wondered if she were still there. Was I talking to myself? "Vicky, are you there?"

"I was just thinking; nothing good comes easy. I'm here."

***

When Anton left for London on business, I contacted an attorney.

I'd found a new tract house on a quiet cul de sac in Sherman Oaks and, on their lawyer's advice, my parents put it in their name. All the homes looked alike but it didn't matter—seven rooms, two and a half baths and a park across the street was fitting for a little boy who needed space.

My parents had always sensed Anton wasn't the answer for me. They never pried, never criticized, never asked for explanations. They seemed to trust me to do what was best. Theirs was unconditional love. Yet it took years for me to see it. I felt such shame inside that I imagined they'd pull out on me if they knew the true nature of my relationship with Vicky.

A stubbornly average Stansbury Street home would perfectly suit the odd little family of Vicky, Joanie and Jerry—to live discreetly and undiscovered by nosy neighbors.

But it was Anton who lived there at first. A few weeks after the move came the California deluge of 1973. The first rainy drive home from work saw my husband storming into the house soaked and angry.

"How could you allow your parents to buy us a house without my consent? I have been on the freeway nearly three hours!"

"Yes, I know, let me make you some hot tea. It's a terrible night." I did care for him. I felt guilty about manipulating him.

"What do you know about it? Maria does all your work. You have no consideration or respect for me. This will never happen again. I work hard, long hours. What do you do? You play all day and all night. You are not wife to me anymore, Joan. We move back to the city, or we are finished!"

"Anton, we could've used *my* parents money for a shack in Beverly Hills or a big home in the Valley. Yes, I made the choice, and this is where I'm living."

"Always you. This is your house, and I'm a guest here." He slammed the door, and revved off. He didn't come back.

***

When Anton actually moved his things out, I was riddled with fear. I didn't realize he would disappear so quickly. A little part of me believed he would never leave me.

I feared he knew about Vicky. He could be meeting with his lawyer already, armed with evidence of his wife's immoral liaison. No such woman would be permitted to mother his son.

I began looking for hidden meaning in conversations about Vicky. One evening, my friend Glenda gossiped in a knowing voice, "I can't imagine what you see in Vicky. We had lunch yesterday, and you should have seen her flirt with the men at the next table. I think she's either a slut or a lesbian."

"Why a lesbian?" I asked innocently.

"Oh, Joanie, it's so obvious she's got a crush on you. Doesn't it make you feel icky? I really think she likes both. I've seen it before. You know how those hippie chicks are. Besides, she's a Capricorn."

"A what?"

"My dear, Capricorns are perfect sexual matches for Scorpios." She winked. Her eyes twinkled. "But you know what Scorpios are known for?"

"That astrology stuff is nonsense," I looked away.

"Scorpios are known to destroy their sexual partners and then hate them for being weak."

"You make me laugh!"

"She'll turn you, she's seductive. I know the type!"

"Hey, Glenda, are there some skeletons in your closet you haven't told me about?"

"*Closet*, my closet? Cute Joanie, cute."

***

My new lifestyle seemed to require that I hide in a whole new way. Instead of putting up a front of perfection and normality, I distanced myself from Judy, Glenda and all my friends from my straight, married days. I still valued Anton and wanted to keep him in my life but far away from the truth. I'd become Joan the Juggler. I wondered how many pieces of myself I would have to drop along the way.

10 A Not-So-Gay Life

After six grueling months, wrung out emotionally by Anton and lawyers, my divorce was final. Vicky was scheduled to move in any minute. I began having feelings of dread. How could I live with her? She was almost a stranger to me. Perhaps another baby to take care of. We'd been seeing each other two years, but I was on my own now and beginning to wonder what I'd done.

"Hi, Vicky," I twisted the phone cord into knots, "I've been thinking. I'd like to re-carpet the house before you come. It'll just take a couple of weeks." I held my breath.

Her voice seemed to fly over the wires, "No way! We've waited all this time for your divorce to be final!"

"But if Maria could stay one more month, to get me and Jerry settled in the house before she goes back to Honduras..."

"I'm not going to be held off, and that's final! Are you having second thoughts?"

"Vicky, think about it. We can't have live-in help with you here."

"If I don't move in now, you'll never see me again!"

"Okay, okay, come right now. I love you."

I sat in the kitchen shaking. She was coming. Right now. I wanted to run, but I held fast to the kitchen table instead. I thought back to my marriage to Anton. *Why am I always having shotgun weddings? What am I doing? Two women living like a couple!* But fear had cost me Cindy. I couldn't let it cost me Vicky.

She arrived a couple of hours later, Bekins movers hot on

her heels. I watched her climb the steps, green plant in hand. With a mixture of tenderness and terror, I gave her a hug.

My official alibi was that she was a roommate, that I hated living alone and needed help with finances and the baby. What a joke! She was practically a child herself. Who would be in charge? How would we arrange our life? Even though I got my way, Anton had really handled things before. Every ship needed a captain!

***

I went to work full time immediately. I was lucky enough to land a position teaching English as a Second Language to children in East L.A. When I walked into class the first morning, Hispanic and Asian kids were running up and down the aisles. Each chattered in his or her own language. *It's like the Tower of Babel*, I chuckled to myself. It was good to be back in front of a class.

"Yo soy, La Maestra, Senora Denson. Buenas dias, estudiantes."

"Buenas dias, Maestra." The sad eyes of the Asian children stared up at me, confused.

I searched the supply bin and fished out some hand puppets.

"What's your name?" I slipped my hand inside the carrot-topped boy puppet and wiggled his body, as he questioned the fuzzy-haired lady puppet I held in the other hand.

"My name is Mrs. Denson," the lady puppet bent into a curtsy before carrot top. The kids had become quiet.

After the puppets spoke back and forth for a while, the children began to catch on. One by one, little pairs of eyes lit up. Each child repeated phrases with me. "What's your name? My name is…." They loved it, and I knew I would love them. This time I wasn't using teaching as an emotional crutch for what was missing in my life. Now the missing piece was sitting in my living room, waiting for me at the end of each day. I was still afraid, but determined to make it work.

***

Within the first few weeks of living together, we settled into a routine. After school, I set the table and cooked dinner. I longed for the days of Maria. Working full time and keeping house was alien to me. I tried to subtly instruct Vicky in the art of cooking.

We stood before the gaping ceramic oven.

"Vicky, watch the way I line the broiler with tin foil. You can put the chicken in this roaster, put in vegetables, potatoes…"

"Really?" She looked bored. She wasn't taking the hint. Her previous culinary endeavors had involved a Hibachi on the balcony. I decided to take a more direct approach.

"Vicky, I need help with shopping and cooking."

"Why didn't you say so? Frankly, I think my meals will be more interesting." I thought of her marijuana salad but stifled a nasty retort. Anything on the table, short of that grass salad, would be a relief after a hard day. So this was what a real partnership felt like.

Miraculously, my parents seemed to take my relationship with Vicky at face value—I'd found a lovely new friend. When they came to visit me in California, we would sometimes go to dinner with Vicky's parents, Lydia and Horace. They liked Vicky, but they thought her society parents were showoffs, too concerned with other people's opinions.

Meanwhile, Vicky had her own problems with her folks. The Bercks had believed her marriage to Greg marked the end of the experimental phase of her life. The move to Sherman Oaks set their world on edge. Bravely, Vicky called them from our new house with an announcement.

"Mom, Dad, I have a family now. Joanie and Jerry are my family. I would like you to welcome us as such. I won't accept any invitation that doesn't include them."

They'd promised to think it over, but an agonizing month passed with no word from them. Vicky pretended everything was okay, but I knew she ached inside. We'd almost given up.

Then they called.

"Hello, this is Mrs. Berck, may I speak to my daughter?"

"Yes, of course, how are you?"

She was annoyed. "Fine dear, may I speak to Vicky?" My heart sank.

"Certainly, I'll call her." I couldn't wait to get off the line, the phone felt dirty. I didn't want to be treated like a freak by this woman or anyone else.

Vicky rushed in, glowing. "They invited us to cocktails and dinner!"

"Great." I didn't relish the idea of socializing with the Bercks.

"My mother said she'd introduce you to her friends as my landlady and roommate. She thinks it'll look appropriate because divorced women need companions until they find another husband. What do you think?"

"I think it's lousy. But I know you need them. Maybe they'll accept us, but I'm telling you right now your mom despises me."

"Look, we struck a compromise. You have no right to be so negative. I don't see you taking any risks around your precious parents. At least I'm honest."

She had me there.

***

We drove in silence through Pacific Palisades to Vicky's parents. I couldn't believe it when we stopped in front of a huge Tudor manor home. "You must have loved it here," I smiled. I knew her folks were wealthy, but I never expected such splendor. *Oh, brother, she's a debutante.*

"It's no big deal," she patted my arm, "my parents are ordinary people."

A uniformed maid escorted us through a marble foyer with vaulted ceilings into the library. Mrs. Berck was perched cross-legged on a silk damask chair. Mr. Berck was standing at the stained-glass window with a drink in his hand. It was like walking onto a stage, and the Bercks had orchestra seats. I couldn't remember my lines.

"Mom and Dad, I'd like you to meet Joan Denson." She gave them each a peck on the cheek. God forbid she should smudge Lydia's make-up. Suddenly Vicky transformed into a bubbly USC sorority girl. I nearly fell over.

No wonder her parents couldn't stand to lose the beautiful daughter they could show off at the "club." But who were they to look down on me? They didn't even know who their daughter really was, let alone know me.

After we sat down, Lydia smiled sweetly at me while her husband poured wine. A vein in her neck throbbed. "Joan, I understand you have a son."

"Yes, he's three. He's quite a handful." Her feigned interest insulted me. I was beginning to feel angry at the way they used their well-mannered veneer like a weapon. These people knew how to make someone feel small, while wearing smiles cast in stone. They were pros, and they didn't fool around.

After an interminable dinner, Vicky's father brought her into the billiard room for a talk. I waited in the huge living room, seated awkwardly in an overstuffed chair, facing Mrs. Berck and her phony smile.

Lydia was even more uncomfortable than I. It seemed hours until Vicky emerged and bid her mother an icy goodbye. "Come on, Joanie, let's go."

"Thank you for the lovely dinner." I received limp handshakes, Vicky's talk hadn't gone well.

"Come on, Joanie," Vicky jerked my arm.

That night in bed I stroked Vicky's head as she lay face down on the pillow, "What's wrong, honey? "What happened in there?"

"You don't want to hear it; it's humiliating for both of us."

"Tell me, for God's sake. What I'll imagine is probably a lot worse."

"It was short and cruel," she had trouble speaking. She took a second, and then it all came pouring out, through spasms of sobs. "My dad said, 'As you have chosen this life, I suggest you seek work elsewhere. Mother and I find your relationship despicable. We thought your marriage had cured this problem. We're devastated to find it has not.' I told him he'd pushed me into that marriage. I shouted at him. Maybe I shouldn't have shouted at him. What do you think?"

"Don't blame yourself; anyone would have shouted."

"Well, I can't work for him anymore. He said he'd give me a small allowance until I got on my feet. 'We aren't trying to punish you, dear.' I wanted to die. I hate their judgmental, pompous attitudes." She buried her tear-stained face in my arms.

"Everything will be just fine," I reassured. But I was terrified. Vicky had no job.

"How could he fire me just like that?"

"He's angry. We'll show them." I displayed false optimism, "You'll find a real career."

"They hate me."

"They don't hate you; they invited us to their home—"

"Big deal," she snorted, "they invited us so he could fire me."

I hugged her. "They can't break us up; we love each other."

I managed to comfort her, but not myself. My worst fear had been realized: Parents would abandon you if they knew the truth.

My second-worst fear was coming into play. How could I support the three of us on my teaching salary? I hadn't ever worried about money until then. Anton's child support was meager, my teaching salary pathetic. Fortunately, my parents helped out when I separated from Anton, but if they discovered the nature of my relationship with Vicky, they'd surely rescind it. Now Vicky wouldn't be bringing in a paycheck.

How could I have let passion drive me into this predicament?

***

Reality hit hard again when it came to our sex life. Except for the first time, we'd always made love in Vicky's apartment.

Thinking all would continue in the same mode, I had accessorized the master bedroom with a mini fridge to provide the ideal romantic environment. The idea was to fill it with Cokes for Vicky's breaks during nightlong lusty marathons to avoid trips downstairs to the kitchen. The bedroom would be an oasis of intimate moments that would make up for the harsh outside world.

However, Jerry climbed out of his crib and into our bed from the start. He must have sensed the change in our household and felt anxious. Would his mommy be the next to leave, following on the heels of his daddy?

Our master bedroom mini refrigerator was never used during steamy encounters. Instead, it stored apple juice and Jell-O. Jerry would arrive, unannounced, in the middle of the night, with his faded blue "blankie." I'd take him into bed, and there he'd be until morning.

One night I tucked him into his bed and joined Vicky in our bedroom. She watched me undress. My pulse soared. She came up behind me and put a hand on my shoulder.

"We can't," I whispered, "he just went to bed." She reached for me. I felt her warm arms and soft lips. But I pushed her away.

"We could close the door," she hissed.

"I don't want him to feel shut out."

"That's great. That's just great!" She stomped into the bathroom and ran the water hard. I put on some old pajamas.

"You know, he's asleep," she called from the bathroom.

"He could wake up and walk right in."

She appeared at the door, wiping her face, "What are we supposed to do?" Her voice grew sarcastic, "I know, I'll set my alarm for 3 AM. How about that?"

"I have to be up at 6!"

She rolled her eyes. "Joanie, if you want a good relationship, you have to keep it alive."

"Good parents put their child's needs before their own."

"Oh, well, then, I guess that ends our sex life."

"Did you ever walk in on your parents having sex? I did-
n't. I never thought my folks even did it."

"Joan, maybe I just don't fit into your life and all its rules
of good parenting."

"Maybe not." I didn't mean it. I didn't even want to say it.
Her own parents made her feel unwanted. Now because I was
angry, I did it, too. It wasn't right.

We got into bed and turned our backs to each other.

*She'll leave for sure…She's used to doing what she wants
when she wants to…She's a kid, she's not a mother…I'll end up
alone…I risked everything for this relationship with her, and
now she's going to leave.*

The minutes passed in silence, then I heard it. The most
beautiful music. "I love you," she grumbled from the far side
of the bed.

"I love you, too."

I'd never felt more married in my life.

***

Vicky and Jerry had other issues to sort out in our new circumstances. She was home now researching new career pos-
sibilities and attending to Jerry, while I taught school full
time. After a long exhausting workday, he would rush into my
arms, screaming "Mommy's home, mommy's home!"

One afternoon, Vicky looked troubled.

"What's wrong, honey?" I asked when Jerry ran inside for
cookies.

"Never mind, it's too petty. I'm embarrassed to tell you."

"No, no, it's important. Go ahead."

She sighed and rubbed her hands over her knees. "Okay,"
she said at last. "I knock myself out taking care of him, then
you walk through the door and his face lights up. He never
does that for me."

"Oh, he's crazy about you!" I reached for her hand.

"Sometimes I feel like a servant or a babysitter. Do you
hate me for saying this?"

I hugged her hard. "Hate you? Never. No one could

appreciate you more. Jerry's going next door to play in 10 minutes, we'll be alone for an hour and I'll show you how much I hate you. Do we have a date?"

"We've got a date." She wrapped me up in her smile. It had been a while since I'd known the joy of that sexy smile.

I stared at my watch, willing those 10 minutes to evaporate. My body tingled.

***

One Friday afternoon, I returned home late. Vicky and Jerry were nowhere to be seen. "Hey, where's my family?"

Vicky's strained voice called down from Jerry's bedroom. I flew upstairs, "What's going on?"

"I don't know. He has no energy, he hasn't eaten, he's been crying for you.

"Why didn't you phone me at work?"

"Could you have come home?"

"No."

"That's why I didn't call."

Damn this new life. If I were still married to Anton with no full-time job, I would've been home.

"Did you take his temperature?"

"Yes, it's normal, but he's not."

We gave him some apple juice, put him to bed and watched him until he stirred around midnight. I had only to touch his face to know he was burning with fever. "I'm calling the hospital right now."

An apathetic voice responded, "A baby with fever, bring him in." "Bring him in!" I shouted into the receiver. "Can't I speak to a doctor now?"

"Stop yelling, Ma'am, bring the baby to the emergency room. That's our policy. Goodbye."

Vicky overheard. "They're crazy. We can't wait to bring his fever down. Let's put him into a cool bath."

I hesitated. "Cool bath? He could get pneumonia and die."

"Joan! Do it, now! Dab water on his back."

We held his limp body in the bathtub. I said prayers under

my breath. Within a half hour, the fever receded. "Get the liquid baby aspirin," Vicky said, "we'll watch him all night."

We took turns standing vigil. The next morning Jerry bounced into our bedroom, fever free.

We took Jerry to the pediatrician that afternoon.

"You did the right thing, Mrs. Denson. Your boy had a 24-hour flu." Dr. Fong looked right past Vicky while congratulating me. I finally understood how she felt. I pressed her hand with gratitude and love for nurturing Jerry as her own.

It would be the first of many times that Vicky would play the invisible parent, a mother with responsibility, but no glory. Fortunately, Jerry's increasing love and dependence on her told the real story. To the world, Jerry Denson was being raised by Anton and Joan Denson. Another parent, with no official title, didn't fit into the picture.

When we'd divorced, Anton had refused to see the baby. Once his anger subsided, he decided he'd like to spend Sundays with Jerry. I was happy that Jerry would be bonding with his father, and it gave Vicky and me an entire day for ourselves.

One Sunday, Anton decided to pick up Jerry early to go camping. Vicky watched them prance down the walk to Anton's car through the bay window and then turned to me with a now familiar "I've been saving this up all week" look. But it wasn't passion on her mind.

"Joanie, I absolutely hate this bed. It's your mattress with Anton, not ours. Who ever heard of two twin beds pushed together? Doesn't the gap in the middle bother you?"

I said nothing while she warmed up to a rant.

"Sure, you probably like it." Now she was inches from my face. "Maybe it kept you away from Anton. Are you still in the business of separation? Because it gives me the creeps to sleep on your ex-husband's mattress!"

I backed away from the harangue and sat on the sofa with the paper. I glanced at the headline, *Nixon Resigns.* A new mattress with all that bedding, that's expensive. *Joan, keep your mouth shut about the money.* "What's the rush?"

"There's never a rush when it comes to my needs, right?"

I eyed her carefully, "What are you talking about?"

"Maybe you haven't made up your mind about us. Maybe you won't be needing a new mattress, huh, Joanie?"

"You're making a big deal out of nothing!" I slammed the paper against the glass coffee table.

"If it concerns you, Jerry or precious Anton, it's important. But if it's me, it can wait."

I just agreed. There was a guilty voice inside me that said she was a little bit right.

I came through the door the next day feeling hot, tired and sweaty. The house was quiet. I prayed Vicky hadn't hit Target again. She spent a fortune there. It was sort of sad—the Saks hippie shopping at Target.

My body ached for a nice long bath, but I knew the two of them would burst through the front door any minute. I sat up and pulled out our checkbook. When we met, I was a housewife with a maid, and I taught for diversion, never considering the money I spent. Now I was the breadwinner, pinching pennies.

But the worst, most distressing part of the picture was that Vicky didn't believe we had the same sexual needs. She considered me a straight woman who'd accidentally fallen in love with her. Maybe it turned her on to think that but for her, I'd be with a man. She knew what went on with Cindy, yet refused to consider it significant.

Her attitude troubled me deeply. There was no question that she loved me, but it seemed that the image of me she held in her mind was that I was a "lady" cut from the same cloth as her mother, Lydia, the Empress. When we made love, Vicky was always the initiator and in true "nice lady fashion," I was expected only to respond. I sensed this wouldn't work for the long haul, and being consistently passive didn't satisfy my urge to give love. It was our last obstacle to real intimacy. We needed a new, more equal bed and a sex life to match.

We got the new bed and initiated it the following Sunday, as Vicky covered my back with kisses while stroking my bottom. "Does that feel good, honey?"

"Of course, it always does." I turned over and took her hands. She gazed at me, confused.

"I want to touch you, the way you touch me."

"But...things are so good..." she started to panic, "aren't you happy with me? Are you tired of being with a woman?"

I held her tightly. "No, just the opposite." I pulled her down next to me and stroked her hair. Her body was rigid. "Just relax, let me do the things to you that you love to do to me."

She looked up at me. "Do you really want to?"

"I'll let you decide."

Her hair fell in flaxen ripples on the pillow. I massaged her back and arms until the tension drained from them. I lay on top of her and began an odyssey from her delicate ears to her baby plump toes. We undulated with deep rhythmic motions, in true sync at last. Her body arched, and then she melted.

My private little universe of Vicky and Jerry was now complete. But an idyllic life never lasts long. After a few contented months, Vicky startled me out of my snug happiness over breakfast.

"You know, honey, we need friends."

"Uh? We...we do?" I stammered.

"Yes, she munched her toast, "friends are important."

Aren't I enough for her? In order to stay undercover, both of us had stopped seeing everyone from our past. I'd forgotten how much Vicky enjoyed socializing. Now we were homebodies, living on a modest income.

Maybe family life is boring her. Maybe I'll have to find us new friends in order to keep her. But were there any other odd people like us in Los Angeles?

Far Out

We all sat cross-legged on a frayed gray carpet in a ramshackle Victorian mansion on East Wilshire Boulevard. I looked around at the other attendees of the lesbian mothers' meeting. Vicky and I had circled the block three times before working up the courage to enter the dilapidated Gay Community Services Center.

I'd discovered it while browsing through the Juno Feminist Bookstore. In its back room was a bulletin board posting workshops. White 3x5 cards announced an Herbal Symposium, an Astrology Reading Seminar, and a Radical Therapy Group run by Dr. Mary Serenity. *A doctor peddling serenity, what a joke.* I'd turned to leave when I saw it:

Lesbian Mothers' Group
Gay Community Services Center
Wednesday, 8 PM

My throat tightened. I'd never seen the word lesbian in print except in an abnormal psychology textbook. How can anyone put "lesbian" in the same sentence as "mother"? That's disgusting! My face felt hot. *Who am I kidding? They're talking about me.* I glared at the index card. *How could they display the word lesbian in public?* It meant horrible things to me. It sent shock waves up my spine, memories of the tribunal at Harcourt, where I'd denied the crime of being a lesbian. Now it seemed homosexuals were calling themselves "gay."

Was it *gay* being an outcast? Was this someone's idea of a joke? Of course, it did sound better than homosexual—and no one knew what it meant; it might be good to have a code word.

I took down the address, careful to check that no one was looking. It had taken great courage to set foot in the bookstore at all. Vicky saw it in the phone book and sent me there as head of our campaign to make new friends. I was scared and reluctant: I would've been happy with just the three of us forever. But I did it for her sake.

I had a plan. First, we'd join the mothers' group at the gay community center. Next, we'd head for NOW. Maybe feminists wouldn't be prejudiced; all we wanted was a normal social life. It never occurred to us to find underground bars. We knew nothing of gay bars, but then we knew nothing of straight bars. Neither of us had ever been inside a bar in our life.

Two young men sat at a folding table in the entry hall of the dilapidated gay community center. One looked surprised and a bit annoyed when we asked for the mothers' group.

"Nope. We don't have anything like that." Dejected, we turned to leave, feeling stupid and out of place. On our way out the door, we heard one of the guys call to us.

"Hey, wait girls!" He waved a piece of paper in the air. "I found the notice. You're in the back room. Follow me."

We were escorted to a shack behind a shack. An obese woman named Rita seemed to be the self-appointed leader. Her blonde hair was close cropped, accenting her overalls and hiking boots. The overalls reminded me of Judy Garland in *Summer Stock,* in which she and Gene Kelly put on a musical show in a barn. Rita, however, bore no resemblance to Judy Garland. She wiped her brow with a Kleenex and told her story. I remembered a couples' encounter group I'd attended with Anton a few years before. Would we be expected to share our private feelings?

"I just got out of Sybil Brand Women's Prison last week. My kid is five, and he's been eating out of garbage cans while I was in jail. We have no money and no place to live, and no one cares."

Vicky went pale.

"What's wrong?" I whispered.

"Let's get out of here!"

I pretended not to hear. These were our new friends, and we were staying put. It was the next woman's turn.

"It's the same with me. My little girl stayed with my mama while I did time for hooking. How's a person with no job 'sposed to take care of her family?"

Everyone murmured her agreement, except Vicky, who began zipping up her jacket. As she reached for her purse, the door opened. Two well-dressed, attractive women about our age came in. I touched Vicky's arm, and we stared at the women with relief. They looked familiar. They looked a lot like us.

The newcomers sat cross-legged on the dingy rug. The tall, sturdy blonde woman spoke, "I'm Shelly. Lisa and I met about five years ago. Our husbands were best friends. Soon we became best friends. Then we fell in love." She laughed. "It's not easy raising three kids. I work for the city, and Lisa teaches. There isn't much money between us." Lisa nodded, a sad smile on her lovely face. "Hey, my dad always said that two can eat as cheap as one if one doesn't eat."

Lisa wasn't amused. Her sad smile remained fixed.

Shelly's announcement that she worked for the city gave Rita the impetus to reprise her desperate circumstances. Shelly was compassionate and not put off by women with whom she had so little in common. Lisa kept staring at us, oblivious to her partner's interaction with Rita. Meeting concluded, we four rose to our feet and sprang to each other like magnets.

Vicky grasped Shelly's shoulder, "I know I've met you before. I remember a party in your home when you were married to Harvey. My husband Greg was Harvey's fraternity brother."

"I don't believe it. You're right; now I remember. The boys are still friends."

"Does Harvey know about you?"

"Sure, he knows everything. He saw us fall in love."

"That must have been hard on him."

"It wasn't easy for anybody"

Lisa was feeling left out. "We're in the Valley, where do you live?"

"We're in Sherman Oaks."

"We're in Encino, practically neighbors. We should get our kids together!" Lisa smiled at Vicky.

On the way home, a police car passed with sirens screeching, lights ablaze.

"Maybe they're coming to arrest us." I winked at Vicky. She didn't react.

"You know, I always thought Shelly was a little tomboyish, even when she was married, but it never occurred to me she was a lesbian.

"Shelly's boyish in a stylish way, like a horsewoman in *Town and Country* magazine."

"So Shelly strikes you as a fashion model." She was sulking now. *God, is she emotional.*

"Look, I only meant she's not strange like those other women. It was so funny the way you almost bolted out of the room."

Vicky stifled a smile. "It wasn't funny to me! What do I have in common with ex-cons whose kids eat out of garbage cans?"

We pulled into the driveway, cleared away Jerry's toys from the carport, and went into the kitchen to heat up some coffee.

"It was such a dreadful place," Vicky winced in disgust, "but we were lucky to meet Lisa and Shelly, don't you think? Lisa is quite pretty. She seems bright, too."

"If she's pretty, she's got to be smart, right?" I punched the seconds on the microwave with excessive force, "Lisa didn't say a word all evening."

"I can tell she's smart. They play bridge. Let's invite them for dinner and bridge. Unless you're a little jealous of Lisa, my love?"

I laid out coffee and butter cookies on the cocktail table

before Vicky's Lazy-Boy chair. "No more than you're annoyed that I like Shelly's horsewoman style."

She didn't take the bait. "We met two nice people the first time out." She took my hand, "There must be others. It was worth the effort, don't you agree?"

"Absolutely." I curled into the leather love seat and propped my feet on the edge of her chair.

We never returned to the gay center's Lesbian Mothers' Group. The following week we began a little bridge group with Lisa and Shelly. But despite our new lesbian friends, I felt a grinding loneliness for my dear friend Judy.

"Joanie, this is your last chance!" She'd shouted during our last phone conversation, "we haven't seen each other in six months! What have you been doing all this time, screwing your brains out in hibernation?" I didn't know what to say to Judy: Fortunately, she didn't wait for an answer.

"Now that you're officially divorced, why don't we all go out together—you and Johnny and Art and me?"

I'd maintained the myth of my married boyfriend throughout my two-year courtship with Vicky. I was bursting to confide in Judy, but I felt ashamed and afraid.

"Johnny's still married but very close to getting a divorce. It's difficult for him to get away to see me."

"Sounds complicated."

"It is."

"How do you like living with Vicky," Judy asked.

"Does she have a special man in her life?"

"Well, yes. (Jerry came to mind.) Yes, she does have a special man who is quite a bit younger."

"That's exciting. Tell me about him."

"I really have to go now, Judy. Let's get together for dinner and catch up."

"When?"

"We'll talk soon."

I have to tell Judy the truth or let her go.

***

I decided to bring up the problem of Judy at our bridge game with Shelly and Lisa.

"You want to tell your straight friend the truth?" Shelly laid aside the deck of cards. "I suggest you get some legal advice from Carter Moran before you come out to anyone."

"Come out?"

"Declare yourself an open homosexual. Carter Moran's a gay attorney. He's very successful; he gets guys out of jail on all kinds of lewd-conduct charges."

"Oh, Shelly, why do you have to scare her like this?" Lisa felt my panic.

Shelly got up, walked away from the table and glanced out the window into the garden. "Because our life's not safe and being realistic is better than living in a dream world. Especially when you're feeling like it's okay to go out and tell strangers you are gay."

"Judy's not a stranger."

"She's not family," Shelly glared at me.

"Have you seen this lawyer?"

"Yes!" She returned to her seat at the table and began shuffling the cards.

"So what does he say about telling people the truth?" I leaned toward her.

"Here's his card." Shelly reached into her purse and handed me an embossed business card. "Make an appointment."

***

The waiting room was dimly lit. The furnishings made me think of photos I'd seen of European brothels. Smoke draped as heavily as the silence that filled the crowded room.

Vicky gave our names to a beautiful, blond male receptionist who couldn't have been more than 21.

We sank into red-velvet chairs. Above us hung a crystal chandelier. Lots of well-dressed guys sat stiffly, holding newspapers in front of their faces. A few wore sunglasses. We were the only women waiting.

It felt like a hours before the blond receptionist said, "Mr. Moran will see you ladies now. Come this way."

Mr. Moran's office was even gaudier than the waiting room. He peered down at us from a desk perched on a dais. The ceiling light illuminated his bald spot and his mammoth Louis XIV desk. Was he trying to be the Wizard of Oz of Law?

"Well girls, how can I help you?"

Unlike his office, Moran appeared quite ordinary. He was dark and trim, with horn-rimmed glasses. His eyes were glued to his departing clerk.

"Our friends thought we should consult you about our legal rights."

He shifted his gaze back to us. "What rights? Are you a lesbian couple?"

"Yes," in unison. Our nervousness made us behave as if we were joined at the hip.

He cleared his throat, "It's simple. You have no civil rights."

"That's impossible," we chimed in together.

"Sorry girls, you came here for the truth." He reached for a diamond-studded pipe and stuffed it with tobacco from a red-velvet pouch. "Homosexual acts are a crime in California, as in most states. The police can burst into your home and arrest you at any time. The Supreme Court has held there's no right to privacy in the case of homosexuality."

The sweet, smoky aroma filled my head. I felt nauseous.

"If the police break in, you can say you're afraid of the dark." He chuckled, gesticulating with the glitsy pipe. "Women get away with more than men. If the cops break in, you can also say that financial necessity forced you into one household. They'll buy that!" He laughed at his own joke. We weren't amused.

"I have a friend, Mr. Moran. She's straight. I want to tell her the truth."

He chewed the pipe stem. "Do you have children, my dear?"

"Yes, one little boy." I held back tears. "My divorce was final months ago."

"So you have an ex-husband. What does he do for a living?"

"CPA."

"That's charming. A nice, conventional guy."

"I was a nice, conventional girl."

"No more, sweetheart. Now you're a criminal in the eyes of the law and disturbed in the eyes of the psychological establishment."

He stood up and walked over so he could look me right in the eye. "So you want to tell your friend the truth? How forthright of you."

"What could that hurt?"

"Let's imagine your husband suspects you're a lesbian, and in the interest of your son, he sues for custody. Does he know your friend? Does he know where you work?" He was unrelenting. I nodded on both counts.

"Perfect setup. First your ex-husband threatens to expose you at the job. Next, his attorney puts your good friend on the stand and asks her if you're a lesbian. You've given her guilty knowledge! You've told her the truth!" Now he was pacing the room.

"She must answer yes or be guilty of perjury. Do you think your friend would perjure herself for you? You risk losing your friend, your child, your job." He turned military style on his heel and returned to his desk.

"Sorry to be the bearer of bad news, girls. Forewarned is forearmed. If you're ever arrested, you know where to find me. The consultation is on the house." He tapped the diamond pipe on a crystal ashtray. "I'm a member of the club, but I don't set up housekeeping with anyone." Moran pressed a button on his phone console. "Women like to nest, too bad."

The blond boy suddenly appeared to show us out.

Moran gave us a parting shot. "Sorry, it's going to be tough sledding girls. Watch your backside."

***

We drove home in silence. It felt like we'd been slapped in the face. No rights, no recourse. I could lose my child and my job.

To hell with the Supreme Court, I wasn't going to lose Vicky and Jerry. I'd kept myself from my homosexuality; I'd find a way to keep the world from it, too. Everyone except Judy.

I broke the silence. "Vicky, I'm still going to tell Judy."

"Are you crazy? You heard what Moran said!"

"I've got to trust somebody. I don't think Anton would sue. He seems to like his freedom."

"It's your choice, but I don't approve of it. Be prepared for rejection—I always liked Judy, but she's a very traditional person."

"I'm traditional, too, remember?" I forced a smile and turned into the driveway.

"You used to be before you became a criminal homosexual!" she teased.

***

I stood alone in the black-and-white tiled foyer of Le Chat Noir Bistro. I'd come late and held back to watch Judy studying her menu. Her charcoal eyes darted from it to her watch. She hated to be kept waiting. *Tonight, you'll wish I'd never shown up.*

I approached the table. She smiled and kissed my cheek. "You bitch, you're late!" She smacked my knuckles with her linen napkin. "I have an exam in the morning. You said you had to talk to me face to face. Here I am awaiting your wedding announcement, and you're late."

Okay, this was the showdown. I would admit everything. Perspiration collected between my breasts. Why couldn't I just perspire under the arms, like normal people? *Because I'm not normal.*

"I tried calling you at the office; you're always in session."

Her voice rose, "Oh please! Don't put it on me! Since you moved in with Vicky, I never hear from you. Are you spending every spare minute with Johnny? Isn't there room in your life for old friends?"

"Yes, there is. My life's been complicated lately. How's the shrink business?"

"I have a few more intern hours before I can sit for my license."

"You'd do anything not to teach French to Beverly Hills delinquents!"

She howled. I loved to see her laugh. *She won't be laughing with me after tonight.*

"My mom thinks I'm a delinquent mother, away from the kids so much. But I had to get away. I had to have a sense of myself."

Boy could I understand that. "So, about Johnny..." I winced when she said it. Judy looked concerned. "Oh Joan. Did he leave? Sometimes guys split when the woman becomes available. Art and I will find you a terrific new husband."

"I'm already married."

"Married? You and Johnny?"

"Married, but not to Johnny, there never was a Johnny."

"Who is it, then?"

"It's Vicky."

"What?" She pushed aside her plate and searched my face. I saw a light go on behind her cool dark eyes. "So, you and Vicky." She looked aghast. My worst fears were realized.

"Yes." I gripped the table; it whirled and I felt faint. She'd walk out and go straight to Anton.

"But why Vicky and not me?" Judy whined.

"What do you mean? I fell in love with her." Of all the responses I'd prepared for, I never would've expected that one. Was she telling me that she, too, was a lesbian? Impossible! Was this Judy's sense of humor?

Maybe it's like I picked Vicky for the cheerleading team and not her.

Judy regained her composure. "Does this mean I'm not your best friend anymore? Vicky is your best friend now, right?" She lowered her eyes and looked away.

"Vicky is my friend the way Art is your friend. You will always be my best friend, Judy."

She flashed her gorgeous smile. She was beginning to get it. "Oh that Vicky. She's something!"

"Now you know," I said.

"But could this be experimental? Like dropping LSD?"

"No. It's been two years."

"Can I tell Art?"

Okay, but no one else. It's dangerous for me."

She looked pensive. "I suppose a lot of people wouldn't understand. I don't totally understand it myself. But I don't have to understand everything now, do I?"

"Just accept that I love Vicky as my partner. I'm still the same as before. Only now I'm happy."

"Actually, I always liked Vicky a lot more than I liked Anton."

"So you and I are still friends?"

"No more lies?"

"No more lies."

"Then of course we're friends."

As we left the restaurant arm in arm, she whispered in my ear, "I hate you for disappearing and not telling me. I was miserable without you. You don't trust anyone, do you?"

"You don't know how hard it is."

She hugged me on the street. It meant more to me than I could say. I was still Judy's best friend.

Lipstick Lesbians

One night our new friends Shelly and Lisa were sitting around the kitchen table with Vicky and me, while I tallied up the bridge games won during the past month, "Shelly and Lisa, 12 games; Vicky and Joanie, 4. The grand total is..."

"Oh, no, here it comes," muttered Vicky.

"Lisa and Shelly are the master players who will be treated to a deluxe dinner at the Taco Bell of their choice." I gathered up the slippery cards.

"Another exciting Friday night," said Shelly. "Are we just becoming boring now, or have we been boring people for a long time?"

"She's right," Vicky jumped in. "This is a claustrophobic life we lead."

My heart sank to hear Vicky's discontent. "We could try to get season tickets to the Music Center," I offered.

"Oh really?" smirked Lisa, "What cloud are you living on? We can't afford a babysitter, let alone the tickets. That was all fine when we had rich husbands."

Shelly began to braid Lisa's luxurious dark ponytail and said, "You know what I think? I think we should do something exciting for once, break out of our mold. Take some risks."

The three of us turned toward her. A wicked smile crossed her face. *Oh brother, what's on her mind?*

***

Vicky slid against me, as Shelly careened her beat-up Chevy Impala around the corner of Reseda and Sherman Way. I looked at the trash in the street and the drunks in the doorways. "How did we end up in this neighborhood?"

"What's the address again?" Shelly called out. Lisa leafed through a battered copy of a gay men's newspaper.

We passed two patrol cars at the curb. "Look at that! This is insane. The police are everywhere. Let's just go get some dinner."

Vicky spotted the place, a shack with a sagging green awning, "1855 Sherman Way."

"Let's take a vote," I implored, "How many want to scrap this idea and go to Bob's Big Boy for strawberry pie?"

Vicky raised one finger, as if bidding at an auction.

Lisa turned around in her seat, "Actually, I'm kind of curious to see what a real lesbian bar looks like."

"Come on, let's go." Shelly was determined. Vicky grabbed my arm and hauled me out of the backseat.

We looked innocent and helpless in the baleful yellow streetlight. I stood my ground while the others walked on. Vicky turned and beckoned, but I shook my head. She threw up her hands in a "What else can I do?" gesture, shrugged and disappeared inside.

I looked at the parked police cruisers. A third one pulled up alongside the other two. I ran to the alley behind the building. I spotted a dumpster and hid behind it. No cops were going to arrest me for lewd behavior. *I won't lose my teaching license for any stupid dance club.*

"Joanie! Where are you?" I heard Shelly shout from the side of the dumpster. "What on earth are you doing?" She knelt beside me and put her arm around my shoulders. "Joanie, patrol cars cruise around bars everywhere, in case a fight breaks out."

"In case a fight breaks out? They fight in lesbian bars?"

"Come on, we're going in there to look around, that's all."

I was mad at Vicky for sending Shelly to check on me. Maybe she's having a good time in the hellhole, I thought. Shelly helped me up, and I followed her through the dingy metal door. Vicky and Lisa were huddled on a wooden bench in the foyer. I shot Vicky an icy glance.

We stood close while Shelly pushed aside the velvet lounge curtain. Inside, we saw shadowy images of female couples dancing to the Bee Gees. I watched a gyrating male couple on the dance floor in awe. *How disgusting! It's one thing for women to dance together, but two men!* Girls hovered around the tables, guzzling beer from cans. I was so distracted by the scene that I didn't see the heavyset woman come up behind us. Her short gray hair looked like a dirty carpet. She glared at our bouffant hairdos and sleeveless dresses

"IDs girls…"

At 35, being asked for an ID put a smile on my face. The compliment was short-lived.

"Love the purses, and the heels are charming," she sneered." Who did this prison matron think she was talking to? Vicky ducked under the bouncer's bulky arm to peek into the club.

That did it. Attila the Hun's sister was fed up. With one sweeping lunge, she pushed us away from the velvet curtain.

"Forget it, you got the wrong club. This isn't your kind of place. The Diamond Club is around the corner, lot's of eligible guys there." She slammed the door, and we stood in the street looking at each other. It had happened so fast, we didn't quite know how we got there.

"The Diamond Club is a pick-up spot for straights," chuckled Shelly. "If we really want to get in here, all we have to do is wear jeans and take off our makeup."

"I'm not dressing like a guy to be acceptable at that dive," I growled.

"Me either," echoed Lisa.

Relieved as I was to be out of there, I couldn't help feeling depressed and defeated. We didn't belong anywhere.

***

The next week we retreated to our old bridge game in the safety of my kitchen, while our children watched *The Brady Bunch* upstairs. In the midst of a hand, Shelly laid down the cards.

"So, did you hear what happened last night?"

We stared and waited. She looked from face to face, relishing the attention.

"There was a murder in the parking lot of the Del Mar Bar."

"Oh, my God!" Lisa tossed her cards aside. "What happened?"

"A woman shot her lover in the head for dancing with another woman." Shelly loved the drama.

I was mortified. "That's it for me, I'm not going to bars anymore. There must be people like us out there who aren't living in the underbelly of the city. Where are the normal ones? What do they do for fun?"

"They hide, like us." Vicky was despondent. We knew hiding was no life at all. We had fought for our freedom, and now we were watching ourselves stagnate.

Shelly and Lisa felt that the solution lay in new careers. Although I was satisfied with my teaching job, they thought that meeting new people and making more money would lead to a more interesting life. We tossed around career fantasies from pancake houses to fleets of catering trucks, but they all required initial capital beyond our means.

Then the following week Shelly and Lisa made an announcement.

"We've signed up for law school!"

"Wonderful!" I said, somewhat startled.

Vicky fell silent. After they left, I found her on the bed, staring at the ceiling.

"What's going on?"

"What do you think?"

I picked up the catalogs that had been accumulating on her nightstand: USC School of Pharmacy, UCLA School of Optometry, University of San Francisco School of Dentistry.

"Forget it, Joanie, I'm too old. We both know that."

"Too old? You're only 32!"

"I've talked to guidance counselors at those schools," she turned away. "As a graduate of Beverly Hills High and USC,

I'm part of the advantaged majority. No equal opportunity female status for me."

I laughed. "Where do you hide your fortune, Miss Advantaged Majority?"

She turned over to bury her head in my lap, fighting a smile at the corners of her mouth. "Stop it, Joanie, this is serious."

She was right. Vicky had the intelligence and the background to do anything she wanted. Instead she was in Sherman Oaks, doing nothing with her mind.

I took her face in my hands. "What do *you* want to do?"

She was astonished. "I think I'd like law school, too."

I handed her the phone. "Call Shelly and Lisa and find out how they did it. There must be student loans out there. I don't care what we have to sacrifice. You're going."

***

And she went. It was that simple. If begging for loans, cajoling cold-hearted bank officials, and cornering chagrined guidance counselors could be called simple. Maybe our struggle to be together had toughened us up. If so, we were going to need a lot more of that toughness.

It was just another Monday family night the first time we saw a pitch for Proposition 6. Vicky had taken a Coke break from torts before resuming the endless cramming that would last all night.

A beautiful face smiled out from the TV and introduced itself as Anita Bryant, former Miss America, current orange juice spokeswoman, and all-around great gal. Everything about her was perfect, as if she were a Barbie Doll.

"Parents, we must protect our innocent children from the pedophiles currently teaching in California schools. We must dismiss gay teachers now. Gays are known to molest children and recruit them into their lifestyle. For the sake of God, country and family, vote yes on Proposition 6."

Fade out Anita Bryant. Fade in American flag.

Jerry looked over at us and then back at the TV. He knew

something was wrong. "Everyone at school calls Timmy O'Brien gay because he's a creep," he offered.

My heart sank. "Why is Timmy a creep?"

"He's always picking his nose and looking at it," he giggled.

My heart sank. I knew I should talk with Jerry about the scapegoating of little Timmy, but I panicked. "Come on, time for bed."

After I tucked him in, I went looking for Vicky.

"You have to talk to him sometime," she spoke from behind the open refrigerator door.

"I know. Not tonight."

I honestly could not bear to tell Jerry what he needed to know. I'd been lulled into a false sense of security when Governor Jerry Brown had signed the consenting-adults act—homosexuality could no longer be grounds for arrest in California. It started to look like America would be dragged out of the Middle Ages, and then I could safely come out to Jerry. Now, out of nowhere came Miss America urging Californians to take away my job. I could soon be an unemployed and unemployable teacher.

The next day, I felt sure everyone at school would be backing away from me uncomfortably. I sat at lunch, as I did everyday, with the same three teachers. We always sat at the same table in the same chairs facing the windows that overlooked the green cement playground and the flagpole.

Lucy McPherson, the second grade teacher, said it first. "Hey, did you see Anita Bryant on TV last night?"

I glared at her, my heart pounding.

"I hope Phil Dorcetti is the first to go; he's such a fairy," Mimi Garnett snickered as she graded papers.

"Absolutely. And what about Margie Peterson and Sue Schneider, those dykes!" Sara Patrisian, my ESL teaching partner, seemed almost titillated. "I'm sure they're lovers, don't you think? Female gym teachers, of course."

I could barely disguise my anger. "How do you know those people are gay? Besides my best friend is a wonderful speech teacher, and she's a lesbian. The system will lose out if they fire her!"

All eyes turned my way. They glared at me for what seemed five minutes. Then Sara asked, "With all the people in the world, Joan, why would you choose to be friends with someone like that?"

***

I was lying face down in the pillows when Vicky entered the bedroom, struggling under an armload of law books.

"Contract law's a bitch! Who cares about the rights of the finder versus the rights of the loser?" She tossed the books on the bed. "Joan, what's wrong?"

"I'll never go back to that school. I hate them all!"

"That Anita Bryant crap?"

"They're all trying to figure out who's gay! It's just a matter of time." Vicky thought for a moment and then shook her head. "Prop 6 might not pass."

"It's been passing in every state. My lunch partners are gestapo informers. 'Look at Joan Denson, she didn't wear a skirt today, she must be a pervert, let's turn her in.'"

"I have some news that might help." Vicky snuggled next to me. "Greg called, just to catch up. He's getting married again."

"Your ex-husband's getting married. What fabulous news!" I pulled the blanket over my head.

"Listen drama queen, he mentioned something that caught my attention. He's become a psychotherapist."

"That's incredible, when did he develop empathy?"

"He's a good salesman, so he probably understands people better than you think. And he's very charming."

"He's charming, great...I almost care!"

"Knock it off. Listen, he loves the work. Didn't you tell me that you always wanted to help people with their problems and make the world a better place?" She sure knew how to get to me.

"If Greg can be a psychotherapist, I can definitely be one.

He's an idiot." I sat up. "But what about tuition?"

"You have a rich uncle." She snuggled closer, pulling at the blanket, "It's freezing in here; are we saving money on heat?"

"I hope your toes fall off! What rich uncle?"

"Uncle Sam is an equal opportunity lender. Greg's in debt up to his eyeballs, but with his degree he won't have a problem paying off his loans."

"My father doesn't believe in debt." I put my arms around her waist.

"That's very noble of him, but he's not in your shoes."

"Okay, okay, I'll apply for a loan. You knew I'd be interested, you wicked wench," I tickled her waist.

"Of course. It's perfect. You can become a therapist, set up your own practice, and screw Anita Bryant."

"I'll pass on Anita, but if you're available, counselor."

"Not now. I have to get some sleep. Tomorrow I have to draft your letter of resignation for the Board of Education. But how will you manage without that terrific retirement benefit at 60?" Vicky was kidding, but it wasn't easy for me to leave a career that had seemed so secure.

Prop 6 was defeated at the polls. Fear of being fired as a deviant, though, had been enough to drive me into a new career, where I thought I'd be safe from the lunchroom bigots.

13 Moving Up

I left teaching to have the freedom to be myself, but I'd chosen another profession where being myself would be too risky. No clinic would train me in psychotherapy if they knew about my lesbianism. It was considered by the psychiatric establishment to be a disorder to be changed through treatment. Even so, I felt like a coward to remain hidden. San Francisco Councilman Harvey Milk's courage in telling the world who he was had been rewarded with a bullet in his head.

So I piled up my student loans, finished my doctoral requirements, and kept my head low. The day we all crowded in front of the board where the results of our Ph.D. exams were posted, I recall asking my classmate Marilyn, "Where are you doing your internship?"

"I'm not sure yet. My father says it's critical to train at a good place. He says the Los Angeles Counseling Center is the best clinic in town."

"How does he know?"

"He's a psychologist."

Adrenaline shot from my stomach to my brain. Marilyn had the inside scoop. I'd developed a strong competitive streak, once I decided to risk everything for my new career. I had to get into a good place.

"Forget it." Rick Larsen was eavesdropping behind us as we walked to our cars. "The Los Angeles Center works you to death. They own you until you finish their program."

An aging hippie named Linda joined in. "I went through their intern evaluation group last spring, and then they turned me down. They're a bunch of snobby matrons who look for their own kind. Don't even apply there unless you're a society girl."

"So what if socialites run the place?" Marilyn's face was getting flushed. "You guys are reverse snobs! They look for talent, Joan, give it a try."

Now I had to do it. No one was going to tell me I couldn't, and I was more than willing to work hard for good training. I needed it. Just the idea of being alone with patients scared me. What would I say to them? What if I made them worse?

**

My application breezed through the Los Angeles Counseling Center, and I found myself accepted to spend every night answering phones, to become "familiarized with the Center's operation." Who were they kidding? We were cheap labor.

Finally, I made it into the infamous Intern Evaluation Group. The "E" group consisted of six weeks of emotional confessions, wherein we bared our souls to enable the Center to evaluate our mental integrity. What kind of nuts would share their darkest truths while being judged for emotional stability?

I told them as little as possible. I'd omitted any reference to a significant other on the entrance application. At the Center, they could decide not to choose me, no explanation necessary. And my entire future hinged on their acceptance. It was no time to risk honesty.

On the first night of E Group, we gathered in a carpeted room filled with some armchairs and a mammoth leather couch. Judging from the oak paneling and framed paintings, the Center received generous contributions. Seven candidates were smiling nervously at each other when I arrived. A phony comradery was developing out of pure fear. You could tell that nobody cared about anything but getting accepted. Our fate rested in the opinion of one person, the group leader. And some leader she was.

An attractive, middle-aged woman wheeled herself into the room, "Hello people, I'm Rhona Blatz, chief clinician at the Center. I'm in this wheelchair due to a disease called myasthenia gravis. It is a progressive disease that is definitely progressing, but don't be deceived; my vision is imperfect, but my hearing is superb. Some people will tell you I've the best therapeutic insights in the city. But I'm not easy." She spun her chair around and quickly rolled out of the room.

Her disability reminded me of my blind dorm mother, Miss Blake, at Harcourt University. I thought about how Cindy and I had deceived her. Here I was on trial again, and it was the same old game.

In my psychology classes leading to this internship, I'd faced a different kind of prejudice. I'd escaped the bigots in the school system and found myself among highly educated people who didn't use ugly words like dyke, fairy or faggot, but threw around "scientific" terms like perverse, deviant and ego disordered with authority. According to code #302.90 in the 1980 *Manual of Diagnostic Disorders*, homosexuality was clearly defined as a mental disorder.

In grad school, when the professor announced in his abnormal psychology lecture that homosexuality was not a viable lifestyle, I'd waited in his office after class and told him my partner was a woman who'd helped me raise my child in such a "non-viable lifestyle" for seven years. The following week he retracted his statement in front of the class "due to some current research." I wanted to kiss him.

Obviously coming out could help others to understand. But this wasn't the safe world of grad school, and there was no way to distinguish who might be enlightened by my experience from who would destroy my life because of it.

***

The evaluation group was a six-week nightmare. Every Tuesday, our leader used a new technique to test our endurance as clinicians. The first week, we took turns telling about ourselves. Easy enough. I wore my demure smile, while harboring a secret vengeance for the world that still required me to fit into the pigeonhole.

Who was Joan Denson? Let's see if they'd buy this: an uncomplicated divorced mother, trying a new career, while waiting for Mr. Right. Rhona Blatz cocked her head in my direction. She wore dark glasses. Was she believing me? I didn't know.

Several would-be interns broke under her scrutiny and cutting remarks. They collected their things, slammed the door and left. The remaining interns grew nervous and competitive, fighting to emerge the strongest in a Darwinian struggle to survive the mental ambushes. Practicing psychotherapy would be a cinch compared to this.

Finally the sixth week arrived. On the last night, our little group stared silently at Rhona, who sat expressionless, behind her dark glasses, until the last victim settled in.

"Here is your clinical assignment: I am your patient; we are in your office, and I've come to say goodbye. I have no hope of recovering from a fatal disease. There is no point in going on. I intend to take my life. Counsel me." The sound of Rhona's fingernails scratching the wooden wheelchair arms sent chills up my back.

A delicate, quiet woman named Kathy, approached Rhona. "Hi," she began in a gentle tone, "I'm glad you came in today because we really do need to talk."

"Well, I'm here," Rhona rapped the armrest impatiently, "aren't you stating the obvious?"

Kathy grew pale, but continued, "You can't forget how much you have to live for. People depend on you…"

"So I'm a valuable functionary. Unless I jump through hoops, I don't matter. Screw you, I don't owe you anything, I just came to say goodbye."

Kathy floundered and sputtered.

"That's enough, Kathy, thank you. Next therapist?"

Each of the remaining candidates attempted to talk Rhona out of suicide. They made good arguments as to how important she was and how much she'd be missed. Her razor tongue slashed through everyone's attempt. I'd never seen her this harsh. I was watching her in disbelief, when suddenly she looked away. It was so quick, and we were all so nervous, perhaps no one else caught it. I saw a look of unmitigated grief wash over her delicate features.

She wasn't playacting. She wanted to die. Suicidal thoughts must have been her constant companion, as she slowly disintegrated in that wheel chair. Most surprising was the awareness that I'd developed affection for this abrasive woman. Like me, she had to hide emotions the world found too ugly to hear.

I threw my pen down and marched up to her chair, holding the arms so she couldn't turn away. "You're making me sick with this stuff, Rhona. I have a deep connection to you, and I hate your self pity."

She looked up in surprise.

"It's beneath you. That wheelchair doesn't mean a thing to me. Stop being a victim! You want to throw a brilliant career down the toilet by killing yourself? Why did you bother living this long, if this is how it's going to end?"

"That's enough, Joan." Rhona's lower lip quivered near my face. I was the only one who saw it. Her face remained immobile.

I sat down, shaking. Why hadn't I been able to control my temper?

How could you lose your cool? I recited the same mantra over and over, the entire drive home. *I've probably blown myself right out of the program.*

***

Our last evening together, we sat in our usual spots.

Before Rhona made her entrance, we all agreed the experience had been a fiasco, and none of us had been accepted. We hadn't remembered enough, listened hard enough or shared sufficient painful childhood memories to qualify as empathetic therapists. Why hadn't I related at least one incident of rape or molestation? I should have made something up to give me more depth.

Rhona rolled herself into the room. One by one she wheeled around the group evaluating each person's performance and the reason they hadn't met her standards. I dreaded the inevitable moment I'd be discarded. Finally, she spun the wheelchair directly in front of Martin Hartman and me, "I have hopes for all of you to eventually become good therapists. However, I'm choosing only Joan and Martin for the Center."

I coughed out my thanks through tears of joy. Martin's face ashened; he appeared stunned.

Rhona continued, "Joan, in the suicide vignette, your feelings were genuine. You didn't ignore my handicap or did you condescend to it. I felt bonded to you and felt perhaps I'd stick around a bit longer. Most importantly—and I want you to remember this because we have something to discuss later—most importantly, your anger came from the heart."

She then spoke with Martin, but I was so overwhelmed to have made it, I'd stopped listening. While Martin thanked her and hurriedly pulled out his keys, eager to escape the solemn room, I didn't see Rhona leaning toward me.

"Joan, I sense there's something you're hiding. If you don't want to tell me, that's your business, but your strength lies in your forthright emotional approach. Do what feels best."

I lowered my head, then tried to speak but I didn't know whether to tell the truth or lie. Which was right? Which was safe?

She spoke evenly, "Consider yourself accepted, nonetheless. The new counselors' group begins Monday." She busied herself, packing folders into her battered black briefcase while Martin breezed past, followed by the disappointed three. She nodded to me and wheeled her way to the door.

"Rhona, I'm a lesbian!" I sputtered, then sat frozen, hands folded, watching the color drain from my knuckles. She stopped and looked up. I expected she'd nail me to the wall for overt dishonesty.

"So that's the secret, huh? That's no big deal, I wouldn't

have held it against you, but I understand the fear. We get lots of gay patients here. Maybe you'll have more empathy than the rest of us, who knows?" With that, she lay her bookbag on her lap and wheeled out of my life.

Out of my life, but never out of my thoughts. I never forgot the lesson of our last moments in that room. For her, being tough didn't mean being unfair; it just meant saying what you felt, no matter who hated you for it. I still believed she was suicidal, and I figured it was the reason she couldn't care less what anybody thought. It was a hard way to become free.

***

I sat in the small lounge first thing Monday morning for the new counselors' group. In addition to the leaders, Mildred and Sandra, there were 10 other trainees, ranging in age from 30 to 60, well dressed and mainstream.

Martin spotted me from the door and rushed over. We were both grateful for a familiar face. Our new instructors greeted us with warm smiles. "Welcome, ladies and gentlemen. The Center welcomes you as counselors in training."

What a difference from Rhona.

"Perhaps you'd like to tell us about yourselves," asked one of the two fashionably dressed leaders.

I was asked to go first. My toes went numb, "I'm divorced with a 10-year-old son. Before entering the psychology field, I taught English as a Second Language in elementary school. My life is pretty conventional except for one thing." I dove off the high board, "My life partner is a woman."

"What does that mean—life partner?" A blonde, *Vogue* type stage-whispered to a friend sitting beside her.

"It means I'm a lesbian," I answered her question. The blonde's eyes widened. Martin momentarily jolted, then studiously picked invisible threads from his woolen slacks.

"How surprising," continued the blonde trainee.

"Why so?" I asked, knowing her intent full well.

"The evaluation group leader should have insisted you be cured of your illness before interning here." She spoke with pompous authority.

"I resent that comment, Trish," rasped a middle-aged, heavyset woman in the group, "My daughter is a lesbian, and she is not the least bit *ill*."

"I'm sorry your daughter's like that, Gloria. But I just don't think lesbians should be responsible for anyone's therapy!" Trish forced her point with exquisite insensitivity.

Our leader, Sandra, rocked vigorously in her white wicker chair. "I'm sure Joan's profile was taken into consideration during the selection process." Sandra's warning tone ended the discussion.

I went right to Mildred and Sandra's office after the meeting, my legs shaking as I closed the door behind me. Now that I'd said it, I panicked. Why did I have to spout out the truth after I'd come so far?

"You need to know that I wasn't up-front in the E Group. I only told Rhona about myself after she'd accepted me. Maybe you better check it out with her. Maybe you'll want to change your minds." I fought back tears.

"Calm down. Rhona already told us exactly what happened," said Sandra. "She thinks you'll be a real asset to the program."

"Maybe you'll raise some consciousness around here," sighed Mildred, sinking into an oversized chair. "We do have some counselors who cling to old attitudes. Change comes about slowly, Joan. Don't be impatient with them. If you take the high road, you can be a catalyst for change. Are you up for the job?"

I nodded. I was still unsure but wouldn't release my grip on this opportunity for anything. It was the best training center in town.

14 Competition

Having a title, Dr. Joan Denson, gave me a new confidence in the world but not in my relationship with Vicky. Since she'd begun law school, Vicky gained a sophistication which, combined with her youthful beauty, made her a sought-after trophy among the social contacts we'd recently acquired.

One night, Shelly wrangled us an invitation to a party given by Inga and Claire, the hottest couple in town. Inga was supposedly a Scandinavian beauty who'd found her way to Hollywood stardom.

"So one of them is a *Cosmo* model and an actress?" I asked Vicky as we walked up the winding path past a dense maze of bushes and trees to the mahogany door.

"That's what Shelly said."

The door opened. An attractive woman greeted us, "Hi, I'm Claire, and you are..."

"Vicky and Joan. We're friends of..."

"Oh, yes, Shelly said you'd be coming." I gave Claire a quick once over, nice looking, but certainly not the *Cosmo* model. She led us into the living room, where other women had gathered around a large brick fireplace. She offered us drinks and pointed us in the direction of chips and avocado dip.

"Dahlings, I'm here!" announced a bubbly voice from the doorway. Every head turned. There stood a willowy, raven-haired young woman with the most piercing eyes I'd ever seen, the color of nutmeg. Her smile lit up the room with teeth so perfect they seemed too luminous to be real. This was the *Cosmo* model, Inga. No doubt about it. She was a walking 8x10 glossy.

"Have you ever seen such a face?" I nudged Vicky. "It's unbelievable she's a lesbian."

"Joanie, sometimes your stereotypes are a joke," Vicky chuckled, "I guess that would mean you must be straight, too." The compliment felt good.

Inga glided through the room, extending one long leg gracefully behind her as she leaned in to kiss her friends. I recalled having seen her photo in magazines.

Finally, she slinked over to us. She looked right past me, as her eyes glued onto Vicky.

"Claire tells me we're neighbors," she put her arm around Vicky's shoulder. "So I'm looking for a bike partner, and you look to be in great shape." Vicky pulled back a little.

Inga clasped her arm, "You do have a bike, don't you, honey?"

"I do," Vicky replied in a flat tone, "but I don't ride much anymore"

"Well, we can fix that," Inga laughed loudly. A few guests turned. She was enjoying the game. "I'll give you a call."

And with that, she melted away, into a new circle of guests eager to soak up the charisma of Miss *Cosmo*.

I flashed back to that New Year's Eve so many years ago at Marcus's house, how it must have felt for Anton when Marcus's sweaty arms had enfolded me. I took Vicky's hand and was relieved by her reassuring squeeze.

After that night, we were invited to Inga and Claire's pool parties religiously. A casual observer would never have imagined the guests were gay. Attractive, masculine men and lovely elegant women cavorted across the exotically landscaped grounds. One needed to look closely to see whether a particular female judge carried a tailored energy or whether a certain chiseled-faced physician leaning against the bar was a trifle effeminate in his speech pattern.

Nothing was obvious. This wasn't the Del Mar Club.

***

In time, we developed into a colorful circle of pioneer lipstick lesbians and gay men, but some of the friendships presented a challenge. Vicky's "harmless" kidding around with attractive women seemed a bit too cozy.

I especially bristled each time Inga sashayed into our living room to pick up Vicky for a bike ride. From her behavior at the pool parties, I knew that the doe-eyed *Cosmo* model had discarded all scruples back in Sweden.

Claire, owner of an exclusive cosmetics salon, had been with Inga for five years. I felt sorry for her; though blonde and perky, she was no showstopper like Inga and no doubt felt she had to put up with the model's outrageous flirtations. I felt even sorrier for myself since Vicky was the current focus of Inga's white heat.

A few days later, Miss *Cosmo* appeared unannounced at our door, "I've found a bike path strewn with wild flowers!" She enunciated each breathless syllable, as if she were rehearsing a tooth paste ad. "Come biking with me next Saturday morning." She looked directly at Vicky.

"Is Claire going?" Vicky seemed nervous.

"Oh, darling, Claire's so busy working; and you have patients, don't you, Joan?"

"Yes, I have patients, and someone has to take Jerry to his science class at the museum." I glanced over at Vicky, hoping she would volunteer.

Inga arranged her hair in the mirror, "What a good therapist and perfect mother. Well, Vicky that leaves just us." Thus began their weekly Saturday bike rides...for health reasons. After all, Vicky needed exercise after those grueling hours of legal briefs, and poor Inga's blood pooled from the strain of sitting around for countless photographs and movie takes.

One morning after their ride, Vicky giggled, "I heard Shelly's got the hots for her secretary."

"Why do you tell me this junk?"

"I thought you'd enjoy a little gossip. Don't be such a prude! Remember, Joanie, you and I never went through a normal adolescence like straight kids, proms, dating, that sort of thing. Maybe she wants to make up for lost time."

"What are you talking about?" I barked. "We were both social butterflies in high school."

"Yes, but I couldn't go to the prom with the person I wanted to be with. I went with Greg, not the prom queen," she laughed.

I stared at her for a moment. "Are you trying to make up for lost time?" My voice trembled. "Is that what you're doing on that bike path every Saturday?" Vicky reached across the table and clasped my hand, "No honey, I'm not making up for lost time. I've married my mother, I could never replace you." She flashed that adorable grin that always made me melt.

"What do you mean by that?"

"Explanations later love, gotta run." She cupped my head and kissed my lips, grabbed her briefcase and disappeared through the garage door.

I put down my coffee cup and held my head in my hands. My stomach churned. I longed for the day Inga would be an aging ingenue, disappearing like her looks, out of our life.

I rarely exhaled during those many months of Vicky's Saturday bike rides. I'd sit after the last patient left, staring out the window of my office, praying she would return to me at the end of the day.

15 Obsession

While we were pushing forward in our separate careers, the shit hit the fan.

"Mommy, do the neighbors think you and Vicky are gay?" Jerry dropped the bomb one night while we were clearing the supper dishes. As a therapist I would have asked, "Jerry, do you think we're gay?" As a frightened lesbian mother I said, "I don't know what the neighbors think. Did someone ask you that?"

"No," said my 11-year-old son, "they haven't asked."

Where had Jerry's question come from? Was it his own curiosity or the effect of a recent onslaught of antigay messages in the media? It really didn't matter. The time had come. The moment I'd dreaded couldn't be avoided any longer.

I hadn't told Jerry the truth for fear that he'd tell his friends, who would surely ridicule him. He'd be an outcast. It would kill me to make my son feel ashamed. I needed help.

Someone recommended Dr. Simone, an older psychologist guru type who ran a lesbian support group. Maybe she could give me some guidance to help me figure out how to tell my son the truth.

I joined eight well-dressed women sitting cross-legged on the blue carpet of a large consultation room. Dr. Simone's earthy style amazed me. She always wore purple sweat suits and Birkenstocks to group. A mass of disheveled silver hair framed her all-seeing, ice-blue eyes. Without pretense, she revealed some of her own personal ordeals during the opening share period.

"Yeah, guess I'm first," said Dr. Simone, "Well, my daughter is getting divorced again. A part of me feels I failed her as a mother; the other part knows I raised her with a lot of love." I felt better that everyone struggled with life, including our therapist.

The next turn revealed a woman who didn't want to commit to her girlfriend. Dr. Simone's blue lasers bore into her. After the woman finished whining about not wanting to be tied down, the doc slouched deeper in her bean bag chair, "I gotta be honest with you. I'm bored. You come back week after week with this same issue. Make up your mind. Shit or get off the pot!"

The group shifted uncomfortably. I was next.

Fearing the same uncompromising directness, I told them about Jerry. Dr. Simone softened a bit. "Joan, people are as sick as their secrets. We'll help prepare you to tell him the truth. Talk to your son. Too much time has gone by already."

"But he's not really ready," I dug in my heels.

"He's plenty ready, but you're not," she chuckled.

"Maybe next year will be better?" I wrestled with her.

"Better for whom? Maybe at his wedding, hum?" she kicked off her sandals. "Don't bullshit me, Joan. You're scared he won't love you anymore. You have to take that risk."

Every week she drilled me. For six months, I sat an imaginary Jerry in the bean bag chair and told him everything. But six months of role-playing could not undo a lifetime of the defenses I'd built to hold onto the people I loved. Finally, Dr. Simone said to "just do it anyway." She couldn't help me anymore. She thought maybe I could learn honesty through sheer force of will. For the first time since I'd met her, I doubted her word.   I drove home that night in tears. I knew what I had to do, and I wasn't ready to do it. I felt abandoned, petrified, but the desperation convinced me I had to act. He was getting older; soon he would find out for himself.

"Jerry?" I knocked quietly on his door, hoping he would be sleeping.

"Yeah? Come in." He flicked off his TV. I stood in the doorway afraid to enter.

"Jerry, remember when you asked me if the neighbors thought Vicky and I were gay?"

"Yeah," His guard went up. I stopped in my tracks and pretended to straighten his dresser drawer. What could I do now? Walk out? It was too late.

I took a deep breath, "Well...we are."

His pale complexion darkened. He started to sob. "No, no, it can't be true." He backed away from me in horror. "Why did you wait so long to tell me? And why are you telling me this stuff now? Have you told my dad? Do Grandpa and Grandma know?"

I left the doorway and sat on his bed. "No, Grandpa and Grandma haven't been told. I'm telling you so we don't have secrets."

His voice came out muffled, soaked in tears and rage, "What, do think I'm stupid? I *know*." He wiped his nose with the back of his hand, "Am I gonna be a homo, too?"

I floundered for what to say, then noticed his walls covered with posters. "Jerry, when you look at those half-naked girls, do you imagine yourself with guys?"

"Of course not!" His face relaxed.

I kneeled in front of him and pushed his hair off his forehead. "Would you rather I hadn't told you?"

He hurled a magazine against the wall. "I'd rather you weren't like that!"

"Do you want Vicky to move out? How can I make it better for you?"

"No, I'd hate that," he shouted. "I love her."

I felt like we were both drowning. "Do you think we should tell your father?"

"No, Daddy couldn't handle it." He suddenly seemed older, encumbered by the weight of my secret. How could I do this to him?

He disappeared into his cavernous closet, and all I could do was watch him escape me, and hope it wasn't for good. After a few minutes, he returned to his bed, still in tears.

"Should we talk to grandma and grandpa?" I sat next to him on his bunk bed and wrapped my arms around his stooped shoulders.

"I don't think they'd understand." He pulled away. "Nobody would understand." He avoided my eyes, "Maybe the Rabbi would."

In the course of his bar mitzvah training, he'd developed an affection and respect for the rabbi. I thought about the party I'd planned. "You know I'm preparing the invitation list for your bar mitzvah party. Maybe you'd prefer I not invite our lesbian friends? I don't want to embarrass you."

"I want all your friends there. I like them all." He covered his tear-stained face with his hands. I put my hand to his back and felt him draw away from my touch. I pulled myself together, "Honey, I picked up cake and ice cream. Why don't you come downstairs for a snack when you get hungry?"

I left his room, and went into the den. Vicky looked up from her legal pad. "Well?"

"It didn't go well. He's very upset." "Do you want me to talk to him?""

"Maybe later, now's not a good time."

Within 15 minutes curly haired, lanky Jerry bounded into the kitchen, where we stuffed our faces with cake, as if it were any other night of the week.

The following afternoon, Jerry and friends came running into the house, up the stairs, past our closed bedroom door and into Jerry's room, as they did every day after school. Why had nothing changed?

"I didn't think he'd bring kids home from school anymore," I whispered to Vicky.

"Yes, that's a good sign, don't you think?"

I gave her a weak smile.

***

I went back to the therapy group and recounted the experience. After all my months of rehearsing and role-playing, nothing had gone as planned. I couldn't have prepared myself for his response. The group members applauded my courage, while Dr. Simone assured me that in time he'd accept me and my lifestyle. Jerry might accept, I thought, but he'd never approve. While my home life had become a jumble, professionally I was taking off. I'd begun seeing a few patients in the house, and Vicky suggested I dive right in and rent an office in a nice building. My dad liked the idea and invested in the practice. His confidence in me felt wonderful.

Miriam wasn't as optimistic. She worried about my leaving the school system, a solid institution, "Think of the retirement pension!" Unfortunately, I secretly shared her doubts. Where would I get referrals? Why would patients call me and not someone else? There were therapist offices on every corner in West Los Angeles. In quiet moments, my fear overwhelmed me. Middle aged and running behind, I was suddenly out there on my own with responsibilities and an overhead.

As a kid, I'd observed my father's success with the use of advertising. Taking a page from his book, I decided to place an ad in the *Gay Community News*: "Dr. Joan Denson, Quality Therapy at Reasonable Fees." A member of the support group was appalled.

"What are you doing, Joan? Selling discount shoes?" Leticia nailed me. She was a glamorous Jamaican woman whose father was, as she told us so often, a successful Brentwood physician. She didn't understand or care about the need to use unorthodox methods to drum up business. I ignored her criticism and plunged ahead.

Through advertising and speaking engagements, my name became familiar to the gay and straight communities…*have mouth, will travel*. Although I battled stage fright, public speaking had always been my tour de force.

I cold-called organizations from the Yellow Pages: "Hello, Mr. Barnett, are you the program chairman of Parents

Without Partners? I'm Dr. Joan Denson, a psychotherapist. I give public-service lectures around town. Next month I'll be in your area, and I'm wondering if there's a special topic of interest to your group."

"Do you know anything about *Finding Love the Second Time Around?*"

"Isn't this amazing? My specialty is love, marriage and remarriage. When does your group meet?"

A successful talk always generated referrals. I was Irving's daughter, no doubt about that. I became the expert on everything from *Keeping Sexuality Alive Within the Committed Relationship*, to *Knowing When You Need More Than a Good Friend.* The '80s therapy boom was in full swing; people wanted to understand themselves, and they wanted help going deeper within from a professional.

The gay center requested a weekly group on the then-controversial issue of "coming out." My stomach cramped up, as I entered the glossy, new high-rise that had become the center's home. It was far cry from the dilapidated Victorian house on East Wilshire that I'd dreaded entering years before. *How can I have the nerve to do a "coming-out" group when I'm not "out" to my ex-husband or my own parents?*

The stark white room smelled of fresh paint and held about 20 people of diverse ages and ethnicities. All the metal chairs were occupied, except the one that I assumed was mine. I sat down and looked at the blank faces encircling me.

"Hi, I'm your facilitator, Joan Denson."

An African-American woman was the first to speak, "A doctor is supposed to lead this group. Are you a doctor?"

"I have a doctorate in clinical psychology."

"You gonna solve our problems, Dr. Hotshot?" A young Latino riveted me with his cold black eyes. "Last year I came out to my folks, and they never want to see me again. I came out to a friend at work, the next day the boss says there's a company cutback, and he needs to lay me off. How do I pay the rent, Dr. Fucking Ph.D.?"

I trembled inside. "What's your name?" "Armando," he smirked.

"Listen, some people will hate you because you're Latino, others will hate you because you're gay and lots of people will hate you because you're both!" Armando smiled a little at that. The only thing I could give this crowd was my own personal truth. It felt wonderful to be up-front with them. The group began making intense eye contact, as I spoke about my own disappointments.

"Some people hate me because I'm Jewish. Last week I lost a patient because her minister didn't approve of my religion. He told her that Jews are sent by the devil, and she'd go straight to hell if she continued in therapy with me."

"That's lousy and stupid," an Asian woman called out. "Some of those ministers are sent by the devil!"

Everyone laughed in agreement.

I spoke of my joys and heartbreaks with an audience that knew well the price of being "different."

"We can't bear the idea of losing the love and respect of our families, and we want to be honest with our friends at work. I don't have the answers, but I'm here to hash it around with you. What's the worse that could happen? Scary stuff, I agree, but there's no air in the closet. People suffocate there."

When it was over, some of them walked me to my car, Armando among them. "You'll be back next week, right Dr. Joan?" He looked a bit sheepish.

"You bet, Armando!" I climbed inside my car and waved goodbye to them at the curb. As I drove up La Brea, I felt exhilaration mingled with tears. *You're a phony, Dr. Denson. They have the honesty to reveal themselves, while you continue to hide.*

16 Green-Eyed Monster

As a self-employed, hot-shot therapist, I couldn't be accused anymore of being a spoiled, stay-at-home wife. I had other problems. My family was on the fast track to oblivion. Somehow, we'd all lost touch with each other. Was the price of success really so high?

A year after my confession to Jerry, as Vicky and I sat with him in Burger King, my son blurted out, "Mom, I want to go to prep school."

"What do you mean?" My shoulders tensed, "What prep school are you thinking about?"

"Mrs. McBride says Graves Academy is the best."

"Graves is on the other side of the country," Vicky said. "There are great prep schools here in California."

"But I want to go to Graves." He seemed determined. "I want the adventure of going away to school."

I snapped. "You'll have adventure when you go away to college." I knew my argument rang hollow. "Jerry, is there something about your life here that's making you want to leave?" I needed to know the truth.

"No, but at Graves I can have my own horse and be in the riding club. You remember that movie, *Taps*, we all saw at the drive-in? It's like being at camp all year long."

"Why don't you research some more prep schools, and we'll talk about it again?" Vicky pulled her best innocent-parent poker face, though she hated this as much as I did. She was a perfect lawyer. Jerry rolled his eyes.

***

When the letter of acceptance arrived from Graves, I freaked.

"Do you really want to go so far away from home?" I heard myself whine out loud. *Why are you leaving me?* I thought.

"Aren't you proud I got in? Come on, Mom, you want me to miss this opportunity? It's a terrific school. Dad says lots of famous people graduated from Graves. Maybe I'll be president some day." He attempted a laugh, avoiding my eyes. Vicky and I pasted on smiles.

That night I begged her to help me say no. "Don't you think he's running away from us? Because he's ashamed we're gay?"

She thought a minute. "You know, maybe so, but this a healthy way to separate. Let's face it, Joan. Both of us are very busy with our careers. You have to let him find himself."

I wanted to hold him and make up for all the time I'd put into anything but loving him. It was too late.

Months later, after Vicky and I'd been left with an empty nest, we sat at the breakfast table in uncomfortable silence. Vicky sopped up the remainder of her straight-up egg on a sliver of toast. Our once-magical Sundays had devolved into a rigid routine.

She grabbed a napkin and wiped her lips, "I'll clean up."

I took her hand and tried to pull her close, "Why don't you let that wait?"

She backed away and took the dishes to the sink. "I don't have time today, there's a stack of files in the den. I begin a new trial in the morning.

"We never spend Sundays together anymore."

We don't spend our Monday, Tuesday, Wednesday or Thursday evenings together anymore either, but do you hear me bitch and complain? Jerry hardly recognized you by the time he left for Graves! No wonder he chose to go out of town to prep school. Probably has your photo in his room to remind him he has a mother."

I stared at her in shock. "Can't you hit harder below the belt?"

"The truth hurts, doesn't it? I accept things the way they are, but not you. You're a bottomless pit of complaints and demands. I don't exist except on Sundays, when you get lonely and horny and have no patients to see. And right now, you're deliberately wasting my time. Try filling your own cup for a change. Go do something with yourself besides work!"

She marched into the den and slammed the door. I wouldn't go crawling after her; she was too unapproachable, too angry.

I knew her advice to "fill your own cup," was actually good, but where to begin?

The telephone interrupted my reflections. At least it was the private line, not another emergency call from a patient. It was Inga's partner, Claire.

"Oh hello, Claire, haven't spoken with you in ages. Yes, I've been pretty busy at my office. How's Inga?" I really didn't give a damn about Inga's welfare, and Claire knew it. "Am I busy right now? No, not really. Vicky's occupied with a big case. Sure, I can meet you for lunch."

She sounded strained; maybe she'd gotten a bad diagnosis from the doctor. So many of my friends had developed breast cancer; it was scary. "Sure, yes, I'll meet you at Le Petit Frite." I left Vicky a note on the refrigerator, as if she'd notice my absence.

***

Claire rose when I approached, and we shook hands. Neither of us was the huggy, kissy type.

I began, "Something's wrong Claire. Are you not well?"

"That's sweet, Joan. It's true, I'm not well, but not in the way you think—and unfortunately, it's contagious. I have bad news for you. I debated whether to tell you, but I just couldn't carry the situation alone anymore."

I was getting her drift, but didn't want to hear it.

Claire folded her hands prissily on the tabletop and leveled her eyes at me. "You work such long hours that I don't think you realize how much time Inga and Vicky spend together."

"Vicky says they ride in the park after dinner and on Saturday afternoons. It's good exercise." I kept rolling my hoop earring back and forth through the lobe, nervously controlling my panic.

"Good exercise! You don't really believe that. If you had been at the party we threw last Friday night, you'd know what I'm talking about."

"I had a late emergency at the office."

"You had an emergency at my place, too, but you were too busy to know it. I walked in on Vicky and Inga kissing! What do you intend to do about it?"

"I intend to talk to Vicky. She's not my prisoner—if she's in love with Inga, she'll tell me." The bluff and bluster belied my humiliation and nausea. Why reveal myself to Claire? The arrival of the waitress gave me a reprieve.

"Are you ready to order?" Claire asked me.

"A tall arsenic cocktail, on the rocks. Make it a double," I snickered.

Claire was not amused.

"I'm sorry, Claire. I need to leave."

Le Petite Frite was within walking distance from the house. I fumbled through my purse for large, black Bollé sunglasses to conceal the tears streaming down my cheeks.

***

At 7:30, Vicky hollered for dinner from the den. "Time to order the pizza." I ordered nothing. At 8, she emerged and bounced down the stairs. "Where's the pizza?"

"At the pizza place."

"Now what's wrong with you?" She noticed the note on the refrigerator telling her I'd gone to lunch with Claire.

"Is something wrong with Claire?"

"Yes, something is really wrong with Claire."

"That's strange, she seemed fine Friday night."

"Really? I guess you were too busy to notice, when she walked in on you and Inga kissing."

"Oh, give me a break! So this is the big deal. A few of us

went into the bedroom to relive the days of playing post office. Sure I kissed Inga. I also kissed Dave Marin, who's never made it with a girl in his life and Austin McBride who revolts me when I'm sober."

"Are you in love with Inga? Tell me the truth. I won't stand in your way."

"No, I'm not in love with Inga," she laughed. "I'm stuck. I'm stuck in love with you, though sometimes I wish I weren't. Sometimes I could wring your stubborn little neck. It's possible that Inga and Claire are on the rocks, and that Claire needs to pin the blame on me. You know, this big case will be finished next week; let's take a long weekend. Do you think you could slip away from the crazies for a few days?"

"It hurts me when you're disrespectful of my patients."

"Oh, stop, you've lost your sense of humor, Joan."

"I guess you'll have to settle for Inga. Obviously, you find her of humor scintillating."

"Knock it off, Joan." Disgusted, she turned away from me and began pulling cold cuts out of the refrigerator.

I walked upstairs silently arguing with myself. Maybe she's telling the truth about Inga. Maybe it was a harmless kiss. Maybe not.

I'm not sure about anything anymore. Maybe I do need to develop some interests besides work and meet new people. I used to like bridge. I could put an ad for bridge players in the *Gay Community News*. No, that's a ridiculous idea. Patients could answer the ad. But I would recognize the callers and if one called, I could explain about the conflict of interest.

How can I socialize? I work every night until late. *You work too much. Stop at 6 one night a week—now, before you become too ugly to leave the house and too old to learn anything new.*

Ma always said good card players never lack friends. I wished Dr. Simone hadn't retired. I wondered what my wise guru would advise. *"Hey, Joan, I gotta be honest with you, this Poor-me crap is really boring. Get a life!"*

17 It Doesn't Pay To Advertise

I placed an ad in a gay newspaper: "Beginning Bridge Group Now Forming; if you have master points and no sense of humor, we are not for you." My first response was from a woman whose major concern was whether my household contained pets.

"Yes, one cat, a beautiful Siamese."

"Oh, no! That's too bad. I'm allergic to cats." She sounded as if I'd told her my house had the plague.

"Maybe the bridge group's not for you." I knew from therapy that most allergy sufferers complained of chronic fatigue, PMS and other maladies indigenous to the lifelong *kvetch* syndrome. Why have to deal with it in my precious free time?

"But we can hold it at my house. I'd really like to learn the game." Her enthusiasm surprised me.

"Okay, fine!" I regretted that comment the moment it fell out of my mouth. Damn it, now I had to drag myself all the way to Glendale to a stranger's house.

Brown stucco shacks dotted the seedy neighborhood. Young hippies from good families had probably once inhabited the area. Now aging hippies on their way down, Hispanics on their way up and assorted homeless people struggled to survive here.

I reached for the *Thomas Guide* behind my seat but remembered I don't know how to read maps. Vicky understood the *Thomas Guide*. She would have found the place in a minute. I groped for the flashlight in my glove compartment. *Sure, illuminate myself as an invitation to the local muggers. This is what I get for putting an ad in the paper. The woman is either the Glendale connection to the Colombian drug ring or a lesbian Lizzie Borden.*

Miriam's maxim that "A cardless life is not worth living," urged me on. There I was driving around in the dark on a work night because of my ma's advice that card playing was the ticket to companionship, especially in the golden years.

"Ah, what have we here, a little gray peeking through the brown?" my hairdresser Maxime had asked a few days earlier. *Loving Care Rinse* had solved the immediate problem but not my escalating panic. If Vicky was really on her way out of my life, what would I do? Who would want a middle-aged lady for a companion? I needed to get back out there before all my hair whitened, dried up and fell out, before I became a pathetic old lesbian, bald and bereft of bridge partners.

No visible house numbers. I'd have to leave the safety of my car to search out the address. Muttering "Stupid, scary, crummy," I stumbled through prickly weeds to a tiny house, set at an angle between a mini-market and a motel.

To the side of the front door stood a claw-footed bathtub painted fluorescent hot pink. Someone had added a sign, "Make love, not war; grow flowers at the door." One scrawny plant huddled inside the tub. *Anyone with this kind of chutzpah must be irreverent and sarcastic, qualities I enjoy in a person.*

If saner, I would have immediately abandoned this venture, but I was a psychotherapist driven by my bridge-playing mommy. I ran a hand along the door in search of the bell. Ouch! A splinter! That's it! I punched the door twice, causing a flurry behind the window. A shadowy image looked out at me from the parted curtains. The door opened and a childlike face appeared, "Hiya, I'm Marsha."

"I'm Dr. Joan Denson. We spoke on the phone." I peered into the darkness. Her face seemed to recede into the shadows. Why was she stepping back from me?

"You have a cat, right?" She inclined her head toward me. The bare lightbulb above the door illuminated her face. Actually, she was rather pleasant looking.

"Right." I could feel my plastic smile.

From the doorway I looked around. The kitchen area was to the left and a dimly lit living room to the right. A cube-shaped, fake-leather sofa filled the center of the room. "Your sofa is incredible, it must be one of a kind."

"Not fancy enough for you, Doc?" she swiped at me with her china-doll face, as she took my jacket to the closet. I'd offended her, and now I'd committed child abuse.

"No, really, it's very practical." I used my best soothing therapist voice.

She turned around and joined the three others seated at the bridge table. I was the fifth, so I had to sit out. I sank into the monstrous sofa, and a sharp pain in my back catapulted me back up. I tried to act casual, crept to the staircase and perched myself on her bottom step.

Near the stairs, a tall glass cabinet displayed novelty sunglasses—Snoopy, Sherlock Holmes, Pluto, Mickey Mouse, Groucho Marx.

Why did she collect cartoon sunglasses? Did she wear them outside the house, perhaps to the market, to school, to social engagements? Would she wear the Groucho glasses, complete with eyebrows and moustache, to my house for bridge if I were to exterminate my poor cat? I imagined my neighbor's astonishment. Such thoughts brought up devilish feelings, and for a moment I wanted to be her accomplice in juvenile rebellion. *I haven't been silly in years.* I remembered the early days when Vicky scared the hell out of me by racing her Fiat through the streets of Beverly Hills at 2 AM. *When did I become so uptight?*

The women in the group were in their 30s. Marsha made no formal introductions. My cockiness dissolved into fear, as I took in their fresh young faces earnestly discussing the failure of the Equal Rights Amendment. How would I fit into this group of young feminist types?

From my seat on the bottom rung of the staircase, I listened to their voices:

"So what do you do? No wait, let me guess. You're a schoolteacher!" said one woman.

"How did you know?" a surprised giggle replied.

Just when I thought the repartee couldn't get more inane, a shorthaired brunette bellowed, "What do you women think of *The Feminine Mystique*? Don't you think Betty speaks for us all?"

A skinny redhead looked up from her banana bit chips, "Oh yes, it's my Bible. I can quote chapter and verse."

"Shall we begin?" Marsha shuffled the deck, "Maybe we should play a few open hands first. I haven't played bridge since high school."

"That's more than I've ever done," the loud-mouth brunette sitting opposite Marsha inflated her braless chest. "But I'm a quick study. Bridge is going to be my game."

I glanced over at Marsha. She was pale, with a Medusa maze of auburn ringlets framing a button-nosed face. Everything about her seemed peculiar in an appealing way. I wondered why she stared downward when she talked to me. *She probably hated me at first sight.*

I figured Marsha to be about 24 and a grad student. No doubt she majored in something to do with socialism and the decline of the West. Her oversized navy sweatshirt hung carelessly over her baggy blue jeans. I had never known anyone to greet a group of strangers, wearing jeans and a sweatshirt. The others looked like they'd come straight from work.

I pulled out a half-dozen copies of *How to Play Bridge* from my purse, "These little paperbacks will help us learn quickly, and they're only $5 each."

Marsha grinned, displaying a dimpled cheek, "Hey, Dr. Denson, what's your profit margin on the books?"

I no longer regretted the sofa comment. The little snot could take care of herself.

"What's with the books?" said the skinny redhead. "This sounds too serious for me. Take my place, Doc."

"My name's Joan." I slid into the chair next to Marsha and

looked across at my partner, a small, blonde business type in a gray polyester suit. To my left sat Trudy, a big woman with a big voice, "Hey, Marsha," she bellowed, "Looks like we're partners tonight." She flashed Marsha a hungry smile.

An hour and a half later, Trudy rose from her seat, stretched and yawned. "Well, women, time to get going. It's been fun. See you all next week." Marsha jumped up and gave Trudy a full-body hug. As each of us filed out the door, Marsha engulfed us all in similar hugs. *Full-body hugs to total strangers? Masking hostility, no doubt.*

I drove down the freeway staring at the fuzzy red taillights in front of me. Suddenly, I realized I'd missed my exit and was now heading for Chinatown. *What am I doing? Strange neighborhoods, new women. They're all so much younger. I don't fit in.*

Vicky was in bed reading when I got home.

"Why the long face? How was the game?" She looked up from the mountain of papers nestled in her lap.

"Wait'll you see Marsha, the cat-hater."

"The hostess?"

"Some hostess! And what scintillating guests. 'Have you read *The Feminine Mystique*?' 'Oh, yes, it's my Bible!'"

Vicky smiled, shifted her glasses and went back to reading. "Forget it, Joanie, you don't need those people."

But the next Tuesday, I was back at Marsha's door. The women were less than interested in our assignment for the week, "responses to a no-trump hand."

Trudy, the loud mouth, sat across from Marsha, "I just love your cute little place. How long have you lived here?"

"Too long," Marsha's cryptic response startled Trudy. Curled up on the lounge chair, waiting my turn to rotate into the game, I enjoyed watching the lesbian mating dance.

"How long have you been playing bridge?" Jody leaned toward me, as she rested her coffee mug on the end table.

Maybe she's making fun of my skills. "I used to play often, but not recently. Matter of fact, I met my partner, Vicky, at a bridge game nearly 20 years ago." The strawberry blonde stared at me, wide eyed. *She's probably figured out my age. How could I have been so stupid?*

Most of the players were between relationships. I'd announced my unavailable status earlier. No one cared.

Marsha rotated to a position directly across from me.

"One no trump." She made a bid and immediately looked up. The lids lifted, revealing eyes of the deepest green. I quickly shifted my eyes down to my cards. Was the long look a seduction or a bridge communication?

As we were preparing to leave, rinsing our coffee mugs at the sink, Marsha tossed some flyers on the kitchen table: *"You are cordially invitation to a picnic at Glendale Park in celebration of Dr. Marsha's graduation from UCLA Graduate School of Physics. (Finally!)"*

"Better late than never," she quipped.

"How old *are* you, Marsha?" asked Trudy.

"Way past the age of innocence, I'll be 42 next month!" she grinned.

Who'd believe it? Single at 42 with such extraordinary physical and mental attributes. She must have intimacy issues. And you have all your issues figured out...right, Dr. Joan? Marsha glanced in my direction. I left without a flyer.

The following week, Marsha took me aside while the others made coffee and laughed over some dumb joke. "Why did you miss my graduation party last Sunday?"

I blurted out, "I didn't think you were serious about inviting me. It seemed like an equal opportunity party."

"I really wanted you there." Her voice became a husky whisper.

I said nothing. Her allure seemed suddenly sinister. Was she the spider and I the fly? The seducer and the seduced, one and the same.

When the group reassembled, my hands felt clammy. Fortunately, it wasn't my turn to shuffle.

18 Deception

While I enjoyed Marsha's attentions, the chasm between Vicky and me widened at home. The bridge game jarred me into reality. I'd been using bridge to find a way out of a relationship that wasn't satisfying my needs. Was I still a kid running away from home? At bridge, 20 years before, I'd found Vicky to be the solution to an unhappy marriage with Anton. Was Marsha to be the answer this time around?

It soon became apparent that the women at Marsha's were more interested in a group share than in a card game. As in most social gatherings of women, lesbians talk about the misdeeds of ex-lovers, and how they, the "good" partners, were always betrayed. "She was some liar, that woman of mine," confessed Marie, the plump school teacher. " Yep, the love of my life fell for a yachtswoman who's now cruising her around the world in a catamaran."

One evening, it was Marsha's turn to reveal herself. She wore a matching Sherlock Holmes hat and sunglass ensemble. "My therapist said I choose flighty women because I'm scared of a real relationship. Next time around I want a woman with both feet on the ground. I'm ready to settle down." Marsha nibbled the plastic rim of her glasses.

A former hippie chic, Marsha had left New Hampshire right after college. She'd rejected the indulged life of a banker's daughter to live entirely by her own wits in California. Most of my girlfriends, straight or lesbian, had married early in life to successful husbands who'd provided them with a comfortable lifestyle. They raised their families and acquired advanced degrees. Marsha was different, and she intrigued me. She'd chosen to struggle on her own, yet retained a remarkable innocence.

Nonetheless, when I pulled into my own garage at night, I was looking forward to climbing into bed with Vicky, safe and comfortable.

But on this night, our house was totally dark. She probably wasn't home yet, I thought. No, she would've said something about her plans. Maybe she was already in bed. "Vicky, are you up there?" I called out.

"Where else?" The voice was not welcoming. My toes went numb. Cautiously, I entered our bedroom. Vicky sat on her side of our king-sized bed, pink granny glasses perched on her nose. The usual mountain of files lay on her lap. *She's really quite adorable,* I thought. I walked toward her. Her face was frozen.

"My replacement just called," she said without looking up. "Your friend Marsha apparently couldn't wait to talk to you after you left."

"What are you talking about?"

"It's on the machine. She wants to take a walk with you on the beach this weekend."

Vicky's anger was barely concealed by her even tone. Why was she making something out of nothing? *Oh, come on, who are you kidding? Marsha's bohemian style intrigues you. Vicky has noticed something going on. She's no fool.* I knew better than to retrieve Marsha's message in front of Vicky. When Vicky showered, I flicked the switch and listened to the soft voice.

"Hiya, I thought you might want to take a walk on the beach Saturday morning. We don't have a chance to get acquainted at the bridge games. Call me when you get home."

I watched Vicky's firm body emerge from the shower clothed only in a delicious lime scent. I wanted to touch a soft shoulder, but I couldn't get near her; she was still furious.

"Honey, that wasn't a romantic message." I reached out for her; she backed away.

"Bullshit! Since when are walks on the beach not romantic?" she nailed me.

"Vicky, you have it all wrong."

She sat on the edge of the bed naked and angry. "You know, I'll only take so much of this crap, and you're about to run out of chances. You're a therapist who doesn't know a damn thing about people!"

She waited for a response, but I didn't know what to say that wouldn't make things worse. She looked away in disgust. "Go walk on the beach if it makes you happy. Just tell that pest to lay off our machine. I don't want her invading my space."

"Okay!"

"I'm not kidding, Joan. Get yourself straightened out!" Vicky glared and left the room. I picked up the phone to return Marsha's call.

***

I was at Marsha's doorstep 10 minutes early and stood outside next to the psychedelic bathtub. A different Marsha opened the door.

This was the banker's daughter. A tight, white, turtleneck sweater clung to her ample breasts. Resisting the urge to stare, I lowered my eyes to her slender waist, accentuated by a shiny gold belt. Black suede jeans outlined perfectly shaped thighs and buttocks. There was no doubt Marsha knew she had a body worth displaying, when and where it suited her. She wore no makeup except for the lightly dusted ruby glow on her creamy cheeks. Her emerald eyes needed no enhancement. Gold and black earrings completed the ensemble. The disheveled ringlets had been brushed into shoulder-length auburn waves. Hers was not the outfit for a stroll on the beach. Maybe we were doing lunch, after all.

I felt myself becoming increasingly anxious. Am I losing control? Marsha's younger, good looking and smart. My breathing became irregular. I was embarrassed. I knew she was noticing me notice her.

It's wrong to be ogling her like this. Vicky would kill me. Don't take the stupid walk. Fake a headache and go home. I quickly shifted my gaze past Marsha's shoulder to that horrible sofa.

She grabbed a jacket and smiled adorably, "Ready?"

We drove to the ocean. Never the Gold's Gym type, a stroll on the beach was more exercise than suited me. The physical activity in my life amounted to leaving my therapist's chair to escort patients in and out of the office.

We parked at the beach and walked along the surf's edge. Here I was, trudging through the sand at 50. This was "getting a life"? My feet became entangled with each stray strand of seaweed, while she pranced lightly over every jagged rock. Marsha slid her arm through mine, cradling it with a firm grip.

With her strong arm to steady me, my clumsiness gave way to incredible buoyancy. The salty air and steady cadence of the waves filled me with abstract yearning.

A moist breeze caressed my face, soothing my apprehensions about Marsha's motives. We were two carefree kids strolling the beach. We glided together, exchanging silly chatter.

"Marsha, do you notice you drop your g's when you talk?"

"Sure I do, but I pick 'em up later."

"You'll never make professor at Cal Tech if you don't enunciate properly," I teased.

She grinned, "Ya wanna bet? You have beautiful lips, Joan. Did you develop them from proper enunciation?" I looked away. "You aren't blushing, are you?"

"I guess people don't say such things to me."

"That's a real shame." I tripped on a sandy mound. Marsha tightened her grip on my arm.

"It's not a shame. It's life," I protested. "You don't understand"

"Maybe I understand too much." She swept a few auburn

strands from her face, "You're a very attractive, unhappy lady."

The compliment delighted me, but I was unnerved by her insight. I felt seen. I felt young. This emotional connection was what I'd known with Cindy so many years ago, and what I'd recently lost with Vicky.

A sudden fog enveloped us. We bent our heads down into the wind. Marsha wrapped her arm around my shoulders in an effort to shield me from the cold. Only a few hours before, I'd planned a short walk and a quick retreat. Now I longed for our time together to go on and on.

By the time Marsha zoomed her Toyota into her carport, I was dreading my afternoon errands and the empty, quiet house after I'd finished my chores. When she asked me in for coffee, I accepted.

The aroma wafted out from the kitchen, and Marsha appeared at the doorway. "Want the 50-cent tour?"

In seconds we were up the staircase to the second floor.

Her bedroom bespoke good taste in the absence of money; I recognized Sears' best fake-wood bedroom set. A frilly canopy, soft and seductively feminine, was the centerpiece of the room. The pastel colors and fuzzy texture of the coverlet reminded me of one of Jerry's baby blankets. Intoxicated with the scent of talcum powder and perfume, I sensed that lingering in this area could prove dangerous.

"Can't wait to see your study," I said, hastily brushing past her on my way out the door.

I regained some composure in the den, while she shuffled through a stack of manuscripts, her eyes partially hidden behind magnifying half glasses. The glasses jolted me into the awareness that Marsha was middle-aged; and for the first time, I noticed her professional demeanor.

The room appeared serious with its antique mahogany desk and beveled-glass bookcase. Sunlight streamed inside through an adjoining patio filled with exotic plants.

"...Then I graduated from MIT, engineering, but there weren't good jobs for women back then. I worked for the

202 • *Except For One Little Problem*

phone company, splicing wires in basements. You would've loved me in my tool belt. Quite a dish!"

The image of fragile Marsha wearing a heavy tool belt, crawling through dark basements disturbed me.

"But I wasn't getting any younger, so I went to UCLA for grad school. I'd always been good in math, and they were looking to take some women in the physics doctoral program. Who would believe I'd be offered a professorship at Cal Tech? I'm set for life."

"Great, just great!" I nodded politely and started to get out of the chair, but her self-disclosure continued with an account of her typical day, "I have breakfast at 7, study 'til noon, a light lunch and more studying until my relaxation break."

"A nap?"

"No, not a nap. I masturbate for 15 minutes to release the tension." All activities carried the same airy nonchalance. She related intimacies with more candor than any of my patients. She was simply reciting her day.

We returned to the kitchen. "Marsha, you don't happen to have a cold drink other than mineral water. I smiled, not wanting to offend her health food sensibilities. She opened the refrigerator door, while I peered inside looking for a Diet Coke or at least some juice. I noticed a nearly empty bottle of orange soda and a half-eaten tuna sandwich I'd brought to bridge the previous Tuesday evening. Puzzled, I asked why she hadn't "thrown out that garbage."

"I don't discard anything you've touched, Joan." Her emerald eyes riveted me.

This wasn't just flattery. It was unabashed adulation, the greatest aphrodisiac.

"Hey, how about a late lunch?" she asked. "There's a cute Mexican restaurant around the corner."

I quickly begged off, feeling disoriented. Driving away, I couldn't help wondering whether she'd run upstairs for her "relaxation break."

Would she think of me?

19 Bursting Point

I often watched Vicky as she slept. Right now, I wished she'd wake, and we'd be back in the days when our love was new—when we clung to each other like two orphan princesses lost in the woods. Now we pretended that we no longer needed to cling. We feigned independence and went different ways, as if we knew our way in the woods.

She finally woke up and joined me after I'd gone downstairs for coffee. I waited for the right moment to tell her, "It's Marsha's birthday next Thursday."

"I'm thrilled. Give her my regards." Vicky sat across from me at the table, her face buried face behind the *Wall Street Journal*.

"I invited her out to dinner." Nothing. It had been six months since the beach walk, and Marsha and I talked on the phone daily. I ignored Vicky's jealous barbs because Marsha seemed to like me, and it felt good. Besides, she needed me. She hadn't grown into her position at Cal Tech yet and was benefiting from my advice.

Vicky and Jerry sure didn't need me anymore. Jerry seemed content with his life at Graves Academy. He'd earned his stripes in the riding club and was keeping serious company with a lovely girl. Both Vicky and Jerry had left my life.

Most Saturdays, Marsha and I browsed through the malls. The morning we shopped for Marsha's graduation outfit was quite special. We headed for the designer section on the second floor of Nordstrom's. I watched her bounce in and out of the dressing room, looking great in everything.

She stopped short in front of a white silk suit, ran her

hands lovingly over the jacket, then began a one-way conversation with the price tag, "Are you kidding me? You have some nerve not to be on sale. You think everyone's a millionaire?"

"Just try it on," I called to her.

When she came out of the dressing room, I gasped, "You're a show stopper!"

"Isn't it too revealing? Tell me the truth."

"Look, straight girls wear sexy stuff all the time. Why shouldn't you? Anyway, it's elegant."

The saleslady appeared at my side. "Does your daughter like the suit?"

I gulped, "Yes, she does." My hands shook, as I reached into my purse and fished out my credit card. Marsha bellowed an objection from the dressing room, as she handed out the suit on its hanger.

"You must forgive my daughter, she's temperamental." I forced a smile.

The saleslady didn't skip a beat as she grabbed the suit and the card.

Marsha emerged from the dressing room. "Joanie, I'm not a charity case," she chided me.

I couldn't tell her the truth. That it was worth it to me to have her need me for something important. "You deserve a beautiful outfit. You've worked hard over the years with no help." I pulled a brush through my hair and stared past her into the mirror, trying to ignore the wrinkles under my eyes.

On the way out, I checked nervously for friends who habituated Nordstrom's on Saturdays. *What would they think if they saw us together, this woman whose baby face belied her age, and me?*

"I have to do something for you, Joan. This was too generous. Next week let me take you out to lunch."

"After I take you for your birthday."

And so it began.

***

After work that Thursday, I crawled through freeway traffic to Marsha's and arrived late. She appeared at the door in a shimmering sleeveless dress. I was dizzy from the smell of her perfume. I couldn't kid myself anymore; this was a date.

A colleague had recommended a fancy French restaurant in the area, but since we'd missed our reservation, the maitre d' escorted us to a lousy table. I was livid.

"Perhaps if Madame had honored her reservation..."

I snapped at him without even thinking. Being on a "date" with Marsha made me edgy.

"It's fine, Joanie." She tried to smooth over the situation. The waiter looked at her gratefully. I shot him a dirty look. A second waiter approached Marsha. "Is Mademoiselle ready to order?" then looked my way, "and Madame?"

My face dropped. Marsha looked pained. I ordered defiantly, "Filet mignon for two and a bottle of Moet!" *Oui, monsieur. I am a rich old sugar mama.*

Marsha launched into a story, talking a mile a minute to smooth over the awkward silence in his wake. I touched her hand. "Thank you."

"For what?"

"For pretending not to notice. For always making it fun to be with you."

"Honestly, I'm not working at making it fun. Being with you is fun. And furthermore, Madame, I've never had champagne before in my life." She glowed, "Joanie, I'm in heaven."

After a sumptuous dinner, I deposited her back at the psychedelic bathtub.

"Drive carefully and thanks again." She smiled and hugged me goodnight.

My thoughts turned to Vicky and I checked my watch. 1 AM! *Oh, God!* I'd always called Vicky if I were to be home later than 11 PM. I should have asked Marsha to phone her and say I was on my way, but I didn't.

So what, I rationalized. Vicky wasn't perfect, after all. There had been a few instances when she'd phone me later than 1 AM about her all-night conferences. Besides, she wouldn't even care. She was probably asleep, exhausted from working on legal briefs.

The moment I walked through the door, Vicky's bared teeth greeted me.

"You rotten bitch, that's it! I'm getting the movers tomorrow. I'll be out by Saturday."

"It's time and a half on weekends, why don't you wait 'til Monday?"

"You think this is funny? You must have been too busy having sex with your girlfriend to give me a call."

"You're wrong, Vicky."

"Spare me the bull. It's over, I'm gone." She stomped into the den and slammed the door.

***

Yet Friday passed normally. We dined with friends. I thanked heaven the storm had passed.

Early Saturday morning, the insistent doorbell jolted us awake. Through the front door peek hole, I saw the distorted face of a hulking Bekin's mover.

"Let them in!" shouted Vicky. She barked orders like a drill sergeant to the men who shoved her belongings into boxes like a sped-up version of *The Three Stooges*. I sat on the couch, stunned. Last to go were a few pieces of furniture.

"I've rented a small place on Wilshire. When I get a larger apartment, I'll take the rest of my stuff." Her comment jolted me into reality. She added testily, "Cheer up, Joan, you can charge me for storage in the meantime."

Within an hour I was alone and terrified. I walked through the house, taking note of missing items and arguing with myself. How could she just walk out of my life after 20 years together because I hadn't been considerate? Does she have the monopoly on flirtations? So she hates my friendship with Marsha. Big deal. I've endured her dates with Inga and haven't made a fuss. Maybe a little fuss sometimes. Okay, so she never stays out past midnight with Inga. Only because Ms.

Cosmo *needs her beauty sleep for early-morning shoots.*

But look what you put Vicky through....What?... I haven't slept with Marsha....Not yet, but it's worse than that....You wanted Vicky to pay for sending you out on your own to "get a life." ...I'm not like that...The hell you're not!

Later that evening, I phoned Marsha and told her Vicky had left me.

"This is unbelievable! How could she do that to you? I'll be right over. Open the garage door for me."

It seemed an odd request. She'd parked on the street the few times she played bridge at my place, and I'd had to imprison allergen-producing Frisky in the attic.

Marsha pulled in next to my white Lincoln, her red Toyota overflowing with textbooks, an overnight case and several shopping bags of food. Everything seemed to be moving too fast.

"Marsha, this is very kind of you, but I have a cupboard filled with canned goods."

"Yes, and some goods they are. You've got a case of Campbell soup, spaghetti with hot dogs, and a loaf of Wonderbread. I'm changing your eating habits as of this minute."

Marsha prepared a vegetarian supper of baked sweet potato pie with bean curd and other healthy delicacies I'd never before tasted.

"Everything was delicious, Marsha. Thank you for caring." I'd pushed the food around the plate to make it look eaten.

"You haven't touched it Joanie; maybe you're too depressed. You need some company tonight?"

Why not? That bitch Vicky has left the field wide open. She's probably using this whole business as an excuse to sleep with Inga.

Marsha bounded upstairs, hung her clothes in Vicky's now-empty closet, changed into a nightshirt and crawled into what had been my and Vicky's bed.

"I have to straighten up a few things downstairs. I'll be up in a few minutes," I called.

I sleepwalked into Vicky's deserted den and closed the door. The cat looked up from the one remaining sofa. I lay down, put my arms around her and fell asleep there in a crumpled heap.

The next morning, Marsha was at the door with a smile. "So you deserted me last night, huh? I made breakfast, come and get it." A glance at the cat prompted an avalanche of sneezes.

"The cat stays." I glared. She cringed and left the room.

I stumbled into the kitchen. "Just coffee, please, Marsha." She'd whipped up whole grain oatmeal with whole grain toast.

"What time will you finish tonight, Joanie?"

"About 6."

"Oh," she was disappointed. "I have to teach from 8:30 'til 10, but I'll be right home after that."

I assumed home now meant my place.

***

As I escorted my last patient through the double doors at 6 PM, I spotted Marsha seated in the waiting room. I froze.

"What are you doing here?" *I don't want her invading me at work.*

"I was in the neighborhood. Ten-thirty seems like forever to wait. Joanie, don't get uptight."

"You'd better step inside my office. This isn't a place for drop-in guests."

"One of Dr. Denson's rigid little rules?" She walked past me and closed the double door behind her. She went right to the window, shut the mini-blinds and turned off the lights. With fury, she pushed me against the wall and hurled herself onto my body, hips grinding.

"This is wrong, Marsha," I gasped.

"I want you, and I want you, now!" Against the stucco wall, in the dark, her hazy form engulfed me. My resistance dissolved as she lowered me down onto the carpet. "What are you...?" She quickly covered my mouth with hers. Lilac scent washed over me. For a moment, I felt Vicky's body and the way she smelled the first time we were together, and in another moment I was back in Cindy's arms. The only two women I'd known.

"I think tonight you'll be waiting up for me, huh?" One last time, she swirled her wet tongue inside my ear before zippering up her sweater. Her nipples remained erect, ready to burst from their confines.

It had been years since I'd felt savage urges. Years since I'd felt feminine and desirable. I hadn't realized until that moment how furious I'd become with Vicky that she'd lost interest in me.

Later that night, Marsha called the house on her way from the university, "Hey, gorgeous, remember me?"

"How could I not?" I smiled.

"After dinner, we'll do it swinging from the chandelier."

"Okay, you're on." She's got to be kidding, I thought. *Maybe not.* I checked out the wires of the large crystal chandelier hanging in the dining room below the staircase.

***

Vicky phoned the following evening. "I'm not screaming, you are!" I yelled into the receiver. I saw Marsha come into earshot. "Couples counseling?" I hissed. "Why didn't I suggest couples counseling? Is that a joke? You, the unavailable hot shot attorney. Oh, just shut up! It's none of your business whether I'm sleeping with Marsha." Out of the corner of my eye, I saw Marsha's hand snake behind the phone table and yank the cord out of the wall. As the line buzzed, I whipped around and glared at her.

"Well, I'm sorry, I just hate the viciousness. Why do you continue to fight with her? Change your phone number, make it unlisted."

Little did she know I'd take any kind of contact with Vicky, that bitch. "Lawyers have a way of getting unlisted numbers" was all I said.

"Joanie, do you miss her? Do you want her back?" I looked away. *Marsha understands me too well. Why do I feel like half a person? It's the dependency relationship I miss, not Vicky.* My psychobabble didn't help soothe me.

***

Happy 50th Birthday! How could I be turning the half-century mark without Vicky beside me? I hid my despair that Vicky hadn't phoned to wish me well. What a vindictive, vicious, mean-spirited person she'd turned out to be.

Marsha made an intimate birthday dinner, but it fell flat. "Surprise birthday girl, I've put champagne on ice just for you." She'd bought a five-dollar bottle of André Champagne. What did she know? She didn't drink.

Her clothes had gradually filled Vicky's closet, but she was still commuting from Glendale. She cornered me over dinner as she poured the cheap bubbly. "We've been together almost two months now. It's hard going back and forth like this, I'm getting worn out."

What's the rush? I thought, but smiled, "Do you think we should combine our lives?"

Idiot! Why did I say that? But without some sort of a commitment, she might never come back. Then I'd be alone forever. *Fifty and alone—what could be worse?*

"What about a commitment ceremony?"

A *commitment* ceremony? Vows, guests, a party? When Vicky moved in, we'd read vows to each other, alone, in our bedroom. They were still in a drawer somewhere. Maybe Vicky took them. *Never, she hates me.*

"Sounds good," I lied.

"And I've been thinking…"

Oh, God, more thinking?

"I don't want to live like a tenant. I have some money saved up, I want to buy into your house so it can be *our* house."

Buy into my house! In 20 years, Vicky had never made such a demand. This is my house.

"Joanie, let's make a fresh start. I want all new dishes, silverware and glasses—our taste, not Vicky's."

But Vicky and I have the same taste. Even at Neiman Marcus you would find the brown earthenware.

"Sure, Marsha, let's share everything," These were my last words before I chugalugged the entire bottle of André.

***

I woke up in an ambulance, Marsha's face hanging over me. A man in white was sticking little, round spongy disks all over my chest.

"You collapsed, Mrs. Denson. *I haven't* been *Mrs. Denson in years.* "Your blood pressure is dangerously low. It may be a heart attack, so we're taking you to Encino Hospital."

"Marsha, call Vicky right away!" My voice sounded muffled as through a tunnel. Would I be dead soon?

Summoned by Marsha, Vicky left her apartment at 2 AM and rushed to the hospital.

"I had a heart attack, Vicky."

"You'd do anything to get attention."

Marsha growled, "Don't talk to her that way."

Vicky shot her a look. I was afraid of what she'd do to her, but she ignored Marsha and continued watching me with condescension. "The doctor said you hyperventilated, then fainted. You're fine. Aside from the fact that you're nuts."

Marsha was dying to assert some authority and some ownership. " This was extremely serious; Joanie collapsed in my arms!"

"How romantic." Vicky leveled a hard, cold eye on me. "Don't even think about calling me again with your problems. I'm dead to you!"

20 Hot Sex Twice a Day

66 I'm so glad you're fine, Joanie." Marsha eased me out of her sporty little car. I felt 2,000 years old. "You really scared me. I'm going to consult my Chinese doctor about herbs for hyperventilation."

Marsha's what I need, I told myself, not Vicky. Marsha is calm and soothing. Vicky is the calm before the storm. *I wonder if Vicky was just blowing smoke about being dead to me?*

"Here are your jams, get right into bed," said Marsha, puffing my pillow. "I'll bring you some of my fresh banana bread and hot tea. I've taken the phone out of the room. No agitating calls for you tonight, my love."

I'll show Vicky. I'll make it work with Marsha. It doesn't matter that her world of neutrons and protons bores me. We can share other interests. With Marsha, what you see is what you get: warm baths, massages, healthy meals and hot sex twice a day.

Vicky and I loved discussing ideas, dissecting our favorite plays and books. We'd end up in intellectual arguments and steamy reconciliations. *I'm glad that's behind me.*

Was Vicky serious about ending contact forever? They'll be no chance to work it out with her if I remain living with Marsha. Maybe Miss Perry Mason wouldn't take me back anyway, no matter what.

It's only fair that I tell Marsha about my ambivalence. I'll talk with her right now. No, maybe later.

Perhaps I'm overestimating my importance to Marsha. I recall the night she carted over her giant photo album. How interesting to see her attractive parents, the sister and brother, the school chums, the academic awards and all the women. The hippie garlands, the peace symbols, the Bob Dillon memorabilia and all those bare-breasted women. There were at least five shots of women Marsha admitted to having slept with. "Sex is fun," she giggled, "you take everything too seriously, Joanie."

"Sex is fun." *I'm just one more conquest. I'll be another photo in the album.* I told myself this, knowing full well her love was genuine.

***

"Marsha, we need to talk," I said the following Sunday, as I scooped up the remaining noodles from the pot of her delicious free-range chicken soup. "I've been thinking we really don't have much in common."

"We both like sex and chicken soup, right?"

I laughed nervously. "Well, it's more serious than that." Her face transformed into that of a solemn child as I continued, "I'm a culture vulture, and you like science fiction. You're just not very sophisticated." *I'm the lowest worm that crawls to be putting the blame on her.*

Instead of taking offense, she pressed herself against me, wrapped her arms around my neck and whispered, "So sophisticate me, Joanie."

***

Monday morning, I watched Marsha adjust the red-plaid backpack she wore to class to the delight of her students. The overstuffed backpack, along with the cartoon sunglasses, told me that Dr. Marsha would remain forever young.

I summoned my tiny reserve of courage, "Marsha, please put the garage remote on the dining room table before you leave."

"Are you saying you don't want me to come back?" Her shoulders slumped.

"We don't work, Marsha. We're not a match." I continued, my voice growing hoarse, "Maybe nothing works for me. Maybe nothing will ever work for me."

For a moment our eyes locked, then she ran upstairs, quickly returning with whatever could be stuffed into two suitcases. She tossed the remote on the table, then paused, "This isn't about having things in common. You're still hung up on Vicky. I've been a complete fool!"

On her way to the garage, she dropped to her knees, sobbing convulsively. I ached to approach, to take her in my arms and comfort her, but I didn't dare.

After her Toyota disappeared around the corner, I pressed the remote and watched the door close on a chapter of my life that was over. I'd been stuck like an insect in a webbed fantasy of eternal youth, when what I wanted and needed was to grow old wrapped in Vicky's arms.

She's probably gone off with Inga. For the first time, I'm alone with no one waiting in the wings.

I took a deep breath and thought about what Dr. Simone would advise. "I gotta be honest with you, Joan. You've been a selfish little shit; but if you love Vicky, you can get her back."

"But how?"

"You're a shrink. Figure it out."

21 | Alone

For the first time, I lived alone. It had been two months since Marsha had left, four since Vicky, and more than a year since Jerry went to private school. I immersed myself in work. Being inside my patients' heads was safer than being inside my own.

Because my "perfect marriage" had failed, I'd pulled away from friends. "The relationship doctor is a fraud," they'd scoff. "She couldn't make a go of her own life." The story I'd told people was that Vicky hated the Valley and had decided to move to Wilshire Boulevard to be closer to work. This had a ring of truth. Like Anton, she'd hated the freeway commute and had often talked of our leaving the Valley when Jerry went away to school.

"Why do we need a big house in the sticks? Both of us work in West L.A."

"Because I own this house outright, and not having a mortgage keeps our expenses down. Vicky, we're luckier than most people."

"Sure, aren't we lucky?" she'd mimic me.

I'd lived in Sherman Oaks for 16 years and didn't want to be uprooted. I hated the idea of change. Hateful or not, change had happened.

The answering machine's blinking light had become the barometer of my well-being. The sight of a zero sent me into despair. This evening I came home to a "four." I would make it through another night.

Beep. "Hi there friend, I miss your lips. I'd love to tell you about my new classes. Are we ever going to talk non-electronically?"

I made sure to leave my messages for Marsha during the day so I'd miss her, avoiding contact that was tempting.

Why didn't Vicky call? What was she doing? We hadn't spoken since my birthday debacle.

Beep. "Hello, Joan, it's Anton. I haven't heard from you in a while. Is something wrong? I got a nice letter from Jerry. He seems happy at school. Let's get together for dinner soon. Give me a call."

For a second, I considered telling Anton everything. We'd remained close friends over the years. Anton never remarried. *He's my truest buddy. I'll beg him to take me back. Stop being a baby, Joan! How many more times are you going to hurt that guy?*

Beep. "Joan, this is your father. Why haven't you returned our calls? What's going on? Contact us immediately!"

I dialed the phone. "Hi, Ma. Yes, I know it's been a long time."

"What's wrong, Joan?" Miriam sounded worried.

"Vicky moved out," I spilled over. "We had a big fight." *I wish I could tell her everything.*

"Calm down, Joan. You can be a very difficult person." Miriam was quick with compliments. "Go apologize to her. Work it out."

It struck me that she never asked questions about the relationship. *Could she know? Impossible!* "Thanks, Ma. Give Dad a kiss."

The final message sent my pulse into orbit. I listened in euphoric disbelief.

Beep. "Hi, Joan, it's me, Vicky. I need to talk to you. Please call the minute you get this message. It's important."

It had been two months since our hospital confrontation. I'd respected her words and stayed away. She couldn't have been more absent if she really had died.

I punched the number she'd recited at the end of the message, her voice breaking. Rattled, I misdialed twice, to the annoyance of a sleepy guy in San Bernardino. *She just wants to retrieve the rest of her things. She and Inga are probably planning to buy a place together on the West Side.*

She answered on the fourth ring, her voice trembling.

"Hi, Vicky."

"Joan, I'm really sorry to barge in on you and Marsha, but something awful's happened, and I don't know where else to turn."

"You aren't barging in on anything. Marsha left two months ago. What's wrong? You sound frightened."

She broke into convulsive sobs. I felt a cold tremor. "Vicky, I have your address. I'll be right over."

I didn't wait for a response. I hung up, grabbed my keys and flew to her high-rise on Wilshire.

Playing For Keeps

I raced down the deserted freeway at midnight, terrified over what could have provoked the desperate call. She must have gotten a terrible diagnosis. Maybe cancer. Please, God, no.

A bleary-eyed clerk at the reception desk instructed me to wait while he phoned upstairs to Vicky Berck. I held my breath, afraid she might refuse to see me. After all, I hadn't actually been invited.

The clerked waved me onto the empty, ornate elevator. Dr. Simone's voice mingled in my head with the Muzak. "You can get her back; figure it out." The high-speed elevator lurched to the 22nd floor, halted and opened abruptly, hurling me into Vicky's arms. We melted together there in the deserted hallway. A quick look at Vicky's swollen eyes and flushed face heightened my fear. Once inside Vicky's apartment, we collapsed entwined on the sofa.

"Honey, honey, what's wrong?" She was pale and thin.

"You came. I didn't really think you'd come. I was so mean at the hospital."

"I love you." I kissed her hair. "I've always loved you. What's wrong?"

"Both my parents are dead." I cringed. "The Palm Springs police called me. Dad's jet crashed into a mountain range. They said there were no survivors." She clung to me. "You're the only one I waned to see." She began softly weeping in my arms. I felt helpless.

"We'll get through it," I heard myself say. "I'll take care of you. I'll keep you safe, honey."

I spent the night rocking Vicky in my arms until she eventually fell asleep. I lay next to her in the dark, picturing Lydia and Horace whom I'd never see again, thinking how final an instant can be.

The next morning I opened up my patient appointment book, went down the line and canceled everyone. Instead of canceling a week, I canceled out the entire month. "I'm really sorry, there's been a death in the family." Vicky had become first on my list of priorities.

I spent that night at her place. We slept like spoons. She woke in tears several times, her body moving closer to mine.

***

Vicky insisted we sit side by side in the lead limousine of the funeral procession. I warned her this could raise eyebrows.

She clutched my hand, "I don't care what they think. You give me comfort."

The sanctuary overflowed with the Berck clan. The cousins crowded into the first few rows, hoping to see and be seen.

"This seems to be the major social event of the season," said Vicky sardonically appraising the mourners.

"Gee, Newport Beach, Palm Desert and Beverly Hills must be deserted this morning," Our smiles met in a brief flash. Together, we avoided her grief.

The rabbi droned "...and Horace Berck, loving husband and father. Long respected as a business executive and true philanthropist in our community, and we will always remember his beautiful wife, Lydia, for her lavish charity events. They leave behind their beloved daughter, Vicky, senior attorney with Berck, Higgins and Kline."

Vicky whispered, "Sounds like someone in his advertising department wrote the eulogy."

Vicky had quickly planned the *shiva* to be catered in the Berck's lush garden, alongside the pool. As the famished mourners gathered around the sumptuous buffet, Vicky shot me a grin, "Reminds me of the cattle call at a cruise ship's midnight buffet," and left my side to shake hands and accept the sympathy of those who'd gathered to say goodbye and feed at the trough.

My sorority girl knew what to say, "Thank you for coming, Judge Berman. My father always spoke highly of you. We missed you and Mrs. Berman at the club's brunch last Sunday."

The grief festivities ended about midnight. I returned with Vicky to her place.

"Could you believe that charade? Thank you for going through it with me." She kissed my cheek. "I know it sounds crazy, but while we were apart, I had Sunday brunches at the club with my folks. Obviously, I was desperate for companionship."

Her sadness had been replaced with artificial cheeriness mixed with cynicism. Suddenly, she saw me as the solution to everything.

"Let's stop this horsing around. Your place or mine?" Vicky winked seductively, tossing her blonde mane in my direction. "It doesn't matter so long as we're together," she said, pulling me closer.

Something didn't seem right. I'd longed for this moment. Now it felt rushed.

"I can't believe you canceled out your month for me. It will give us time to put our lives back in order."

"Honey, there's nothing I want more. The thing is, I know you're grief-stricken."

"Baloney," she turned away defiantly, "they never loved or accepted me. The great philanthropist hardly gave me a dime when he learned I hadn't been cured of my affliction. You're the one who put me through law school."

"But, honey, they loved you and were proud of you. They didn't understand you, but they loved you. I know it."

"I wish I could know it. Well, if you say I'm grief stricken, it must be true. You're the shrink. All the more reason for us to be together."

"I'll be with you everyday, but I want you to have some time to think and be with yourself. When people feel scared and empty, they can make decisions they later regret."

"Like you and Marsha?" Her eyes hardened. The hurt was still there.

"Yes, like Marsha and me. Be with yourself, and really think about us."

I couldn't believe I was selling the idea of living alone for personal growth. The one who had been forever afraid of the dark.

Vicky entered grief therapy with a colleague of mine. We saw each other daily for limited periods of time. I began to cut back my practice by not accepting new patients. Vicky and I agreed that career demands wouldn't consume us, as before.

***

Her forced smile at dinner told me she'd been through a wringer of tears. Vicky needed to talk about her childhood, both the miserable and the pleasant memories. How Horace and Lydia had cheered her success on the tennis team and their pride in her academic achievements. "It's funny. I'm learning to be grateful for the good stuff they tried to do when I was little."

"The stuff that created your inflated ego?" I teased.

"Yes," she smiled, "I'm free now. I don't have to prove anything to anyone anymore."

***

Several weeks later, we dined together in a pink-and-green upholstered booth in the Polo Lounge. Vicky handed me a small, carefully wrapped silver box.

"What's the occasion?"

"Just open it." Her eyes widened with anticipation.

A brilliant diamond wedding band stared up at me. I gripped the thick napkin on my lap.

"Is this a proposal?" I grinned.

"Well, will you?" she asked nervously.

"Yes, I will, of course I will."

***

We talked, returning to her apartment later that evening. "Joanie, I still remember that relationship lecture of yours, and now it's time to practice what you preach. Remember the triple A's? 'Affection, Affirmation and Appreciation'?"

"Sure, that was my most successful workshop. Too bad I didn't apply those tenets in my own life." I thought of how badly we'd messed up.

"Well, I'm willing to spend my entire inheritance on marital therapy," Vicky chuckled, enfolding my arm in hers and guiding me across the living room to the balcony. The night was balmy, as we stepped out onto the green tiles. "Wouldn't Horace and Lydia love it? Speaking of spending my inheritance, I have a requirement, too," she grinned that delicious sly grin that always made me melt on the spot.

"What do you mean, honey?" My stomach cramped. Vicky leaned against the rail, enjoying the shimmering skyline of Century City.

"Joanie, you've been so ecstatic about this apartment's gorgeous view that I've been thinking maybe we could buy a condo together with a panoramic vista."

"Hey, slow down, counselor. I'm terrified of not owning a house of my own." Turning from the view, walking back inside, my anxieties argued against her proposal. *If we owned a place together, we'd be joint tenants. Goodbye, sole owner. Even the words resonate differently. Sole owner has a mellifluous sound, whereas joint tenants has an ugly, dissonant ring.*

Being sole owner is prudent, sensible. Who can predict the future? Vicky could run off with someone new and force the sale of the house. I could end up an old, homeless bag lady.

I poured two glasses of Merlot. Vicky lifted her glass, "A toast to our joint home ownership and a commitment ceremony up the road."

"Yes, up the road." I stared into my glass. Was I looking for a way out?

Vicky took the empty wine glass from my hand and placed it on the tray. "Honey, I've missed you so much it hurts." She kissed my neck, and I felt the hardness and softness of her body against mine. We trembled together, floating and weightless. Nothing mattered. Nothing.

***

The sharp ring of the phone intruded into my reverie of the night's frenzied pleasures, as I rinsed breakfast dishes in Vicky's kitchen. She'd left for work around 8. I rubbed a soapy hand across my jeans and lifted the receiver.

"Hi, guess what?" Vicky sounded radiant. "Our new governor signed a domestic partnership bill this morning! Now we can make that ring official."

"That's great. Good for Gray Davis!" I suddenly felt the room spin. "We'll talk about it when you get home tonight."

***

After dinner, we sat together on a love seat by the fireplace. "This news is so wonderful. With the new law, we won't have to worry about being barred from access at the hospital. We might even be able to get family benefits." She stretched a perfumed arm across my shoulders and pressed me close. I felt cradled in a bed of gardenias. "I think the minute we're able to register as domestic partners we should have a public commitment ceremony in a fancy hotel and make it the closest thing to a wedding."

I didn't know what to say. I didn't want to stand up in public at a *wedding*.

I knew she deserved the truth after everything we'd been through, so I just said it. "You can't expect me to get out in front of everyone, just like that. It's okay for you, your parents are dead." *That was below the belt.* The silence scared me.

Vicky put her hands over her eyes and rocked back and forth, stifling a heavy moan. "How could you? I came out to my parents long before they died, remember?"

"Honey, I didn't mean to be unkind, but that was then, and this is now! My parents are alive. My son, our son, is very much alive. What will going public do to him? My parents have always been good to me; do you expect me to spit in their faces?"

Vicky stood, hands on hips, eager to engage me. "Why do you have to protect them from who and what you are? Are you so despicable? Is this lifestyle so disgusting?"

"Yes, Godamnit! It is." I hissed, "Everyone hates homos, and you know it."

"Sounds like you're leading the charge." Vicky grasped the fireplace mantel, as though I'd kicked all the air out of her.

I continued my harangue, "I'm not the hero you are, okay? And I don't see what good your honesty with your folks did. They barely tolerated us. Do you want me to go through that with my parents? I can't, I can't do it." Tears gushed down my face. "It would kill me if they didn't love me anymore."

She looked defeated, and turned her back. "I'm sorry, but you sound five years old."

"It's just the public ceremony, honey, please. I'm afraid."

"I never realized what a child you are. You're a spoiled little girl, and you've swallowed the world's prejudice."

"You haven't heard a word I've said. How can you want to force me into something I don't want?"

"Don't want—or are too much of a coward to want?"

"How dare you call me a coward!" I hurled a sofa pillow at her head. She caught it midair. "I thought you really loved me, but now I see you're a bundle of dangerous demands! I'm going back to my own house." I dashed into the bathroom and swept my cosmetics into a sports bag.

Vicky followed, "Oh, how professional, just watch the consultant on family issues run away."

"Yes, I am an expert, and I'm protecting my profession. I have to be on Matt Collins's talk show next week, and the last thing I need is to be questioned about my domestic partnership."

"How sweet, the closet queen is going to lecture the house-wives on the joys of family union. I'll be sure to tune in!"

"Don't do me any favors." I slammed the front door and bolted for the elevator.

***

"Good afternoon, friends, this is Matt Collins with *Today in L.A.* I'd like to welcome to our studio Dr. Joan Denson, a respected family counselor in private practice and hospital consultant in the field of marital therapy."

"Thank you, Matt."

"Our discussion today considers the question: 'What will become of the American family as we know it, in the 21st century?' More unmarried women are choosing to have babies, men are raising children without wives, and more people are just are living together outside of wedlock than ever before. Just where are we heading, Doctor Joan?"

"Matt, since the time we broke away from the arranged marriage, the foundation of the family has been love. So the structure itself may not be relevant. We can no longer try to limit the definition of family by saying everyone must adhere to a certain standard. Life isn't as simple as the unrealistic ideal of the 1950's nuclear family. To my mind, where love is present, all is possible."

"Let's see if our listeners agree."

"Jean from Nebraska, what is your question?"

"I don't see why young women can't just get married and stay home with their kids like they used to." I heard the dry cornfields in her voice. "Why do today's kids have to be different with their pierced noses and illegitimate babies? It all goes together, don't you think?"

"Today's kids seem pretty foreign to us, don't they, Jean?" *This show is a piece of cake…* "90 percent of the wives in America today work full time. Both men and women have more options. Some young women are lost, but others are studying to be doctors, lawyers, architects, where once they felt secretarial school was the highest career rung possible."

"Because they don't give a hoot about the family. They're just trying to satisfy themselves."

"Most women have to work because it takes two incomes to support a family nowadays. Is that selfishness?"

"It's greed. And it can't be working because everyone's getting divorced."

"Thanks, Jean." Bill snapped her off. "Hello, Tom from Colorado, what is your question for Dr. Joan?"

"Doctor, don't you think the justice system conspires to destroy the modern family?"

Oh, no! *Please don't let him go where I think he's headed.*

"Look at what just happened in Vermont. The Vermont Supreme Court ruled that gays have the right to marry. We all know the Court was under the gun from gay terrorists. These people are sinners, who should be put in mental hospitals like drug addicts, not marching down the aisle like God-fearing normal people—"

"Do you have a question for Dr. Denson?" Matt interrupted. I clinched my jaw.

"Doctor, what exactly do you think about queers getting married?"

I gulped, my stomach meshed into one singular knot.

"In my opinion," I hesitated, "people don't choose their sexual orientation. It chooses them. Did you make a decision to be straight, or did you just know you had an eye for the girls?"

"Sure I knew since I was a kid. No doubts about it." Tom chortled his manliness.

"Right, and more and more we're learning that it's a matter of biology, not choice. But even if it were simply a choice, isn't that one of the basic freedoms we hold dear?"

"Sounds to me like you're saying it's okay for queers to get married. What if it was someone in *your* family, Doc?"

"Actually, Tom," I heard myself saying, "there is someone in my family...and...it's me."

Cut to commercial.

Matt fell back in his chair, stricken. His neck flushed red. "I wish I'd known this before we went on the air!"

"Honestly, Matt, you don't know how long I've stayed quiet. I didn't intend to come out now, or ever, but the hate...his hatred....made me snap back with the truth."

Meeting my agonized eyes, he said gently, "That must have been rough for you. I'm going to have our secretary screen the rest of the calls."

Heavy with defeat, I trudged up each stair of my Sherman Oaks home, as the phone began to ring. *Leave me alone. I never want to see or talk to anyone ever again. My life is over.*

Beep. "It's Vicky, pick up. I know you're there." She sounded simultaneously irritated and happy. I held the phone to my ear, silently listening. "I can't believe you. Some nobody on a telephone gets you to come out on the radio! On syndicated radio! And I can't get you to agree to a quiet little commitment ceremony at a very private party in a teeny-weeny hotel!" Click. A few minutes passed, and the phone rang again.

This time I answered, "All right, keep shooting. What else?"

"How'd you know it was me?" Vicky's tone held a smile.

"I'm psychic or haven't you noticed? What do you want, now?"

"I wanted to apologize for being a jerk." Her voice lowered into a throaty whisper, "Joanie, it took such guts to do what you did. I'm proud of you. Really proud."

66"The receptionist just called that there's a limo down-stairs. Art, did you order a limo?" I questioned my friend Judy's husband. They were both sitting in our living room, dressed to kill. Art shrugged, I turned to Vicky.

"Nothing but the best for us," she beamed. *Everyone in the lobby will notice us leave in a limo. Two women in white dresses, what will they think? She's savoring every moment of this craziness.*

"It isn't everyday a girl gets married." Vicky gave herself an admiring look in the hall mirror. "Well, how do I look?"

"Like something out of *Modern Bride*." I forced a smile.

"Not the image I was trying to create," she smirked.

"I know the image, honey—simple sophistication and you've got it."

"Oh, my God, there's a bulge around my stomach," Vicky frowned, "This stupid body suit isn't doing its job."

"You're an 8x10 glossy." I felt awe mixed with desire.

"And what about you? I've never seen you in white velvet. Wow!" She pulled me into the bedroom, where she unearthed a large white box from her dressing room closet. "Look, I bought us a couple of quaint veils."

"Is the Ayatollah Khomeini attending?"

Vicky carefully placed the veil crowns on both our heads.

I ran to the bathroom mirror, "This is ridiculous! It makes me look like I'm wearing a Halloween costume." I tossed the veil on the bed. She retrieved it, as we returned to the living room.

"Art, I heard the phone ring. Is Jerry on his way up?" My stomach wrenched. *How would my son react to all of this?*

"No, he called from his car. He'll be here in a few minutes." Art seemed nervous.

"How do I look?" Judy asked her husband. "Never mind—I know I look fabulous."

Judy held my shoulder as she struggled into her new suede pumps, "These damn things hurt already. I never imagined when I first met you and Anton that I'd end up matron of honor at a dyke wedding."

Vicky and I exchanged a stunned look. "And Joan never imagined she'd hear such homophobia whistling through those sparkling white dentures." Vicky tossed her head, turned and left the room.

I ran after her into the bedroom, "Oh, honey, even my closest friend is uncomfortable. Please, let's forget the ceremony and just sit down to a nice dinner with our friends."

"Judy has a sick sense of humor," she huffed.

Judy came in looking sheepish and closed the door. "Joanie, I'm so sorry for making fun of you. I didn't mean it."

"No, you're right on target. That's how everybody feels. If my best friend is laughing, everyone will be in stitches. I'm not leaving this room."

Judy sat on the bed and spoke in a serious tone, so unlike her usual irreverent manner, that even Vicky looked surprised. "Joan, your mom once told me her parents refused to give her a wedding because they disapproved of your dad being a poor boy. But she didn't give a hoot what anyone thought. She went out and eloped. So hold your head up and be proud of your love." Her lower lip quivered. "I'm ashamed to have hurt you with my smart-aleck comment. Can you forgive me?" I hugged her so hard we both cried, and Vicky wrapped her arms around the two of us.

"Hey, where is everybody? Art's drinking all the champagne out here!" Jerry's voice drew us to the living room. Vicky and Judy descended on him, marking each cheek with lipsticked kisses, while he adjusted his cummerbund in the mirror.

He eyed me disapprovingly, "Really, Mom, couldn't you two manage without the white dresses? Good thing I didn't invite my girlfriend."

"You see, he's ashamed of me," I blurted out, but the phone interrupted our exchange. Jerry picked it up automatically, "Hello. Oh, hi Grandma. Yeah, I'm here. We were just heading out to the big party. What party?" He shot me a smug look, "I'll let you talk to Mom. She'll tell you all about it." He tossed me the phone.

"Oh, hi, Ma."

"What's wrong with Jerry? Why was he so abrupt?" Miriam didn't miss a beat.

"He's in a dark mood this evening."

"Did he bring his girlfriend?"

"No, he didn't. No, they haven't broken up. He just doesn't bring her around much."

"Why?"

"Why—I guess he's afraid she'll think we're gay."

"Well, everyone knows that!" I didn't trust my ears.

"How's Dad feeling?" *Stop avoiding the truth.* "Ma, actually we're not going to an ordinary party. We're giving the party, and Vicky and I are having a commitment ceremony with a rabbi."

"What are you wearing?"

"A white velvet dress."

"Very nice. Don't forget to send photos."

I can't believe I'm having this conversation.

"I love you, Ma. Give Dad a kiss from both of us. Yes, I'll tell Jerry to stop acting like a jerk." I looked him in the eye.

Then I went to the bathroom and sat down on the edge of the tub, overwhelmed. All this time, they'd known. And they loved me anyway. We had lost so many years covering it up. My shame had blinded me to their unconditional love.

***

Our bridal party of five piled into the Rolls-Royce stretch limo. "This is cool, really cool!" Jerry suddenly came alive.

No one can see me through these darkened windows, yet I see everyone. Exactly the way my life has been all these years. The sleek limo crept up Sunset Boulevard, until we saw the hotel looming ahead. All our old friends stood outside: Glenda and Zev, Inga and Claire, Susie and Franz, Shelly and Lisa. My stomach rumbled out loud.

Judy's dark eyes twinkled at my panicked expression. "Joan, stop acting like you're the only bride in this limo. Jerry, slap a smile on your face! Art, straighten your bow tie."

We struggled out of the car, and were met with flashing cameras as if we were movie stars.

Inside the lush penthouse ballroom we settled into our seats. Jerry, Judy and Art and a few close friends joined us at the head table. I extended my arms and offered some stiff hugs, "We're glad you could come." The guests looked as anxious as I felt. Jerry shook hands with well-wishers, his face flushed with embarrassment. I couldn't fault him for his shame; I'd been his best teacher.

"Why are straights seated at the same tables with the gays?" I whispered to Vicky, trying to conceal my panic.

She shifted away from me, "Why not make friends of strangers?"

Maybe she was right. I looked around at the 12 candlelit tables illuminating a cordiality that surprised me. People were actually talking to each other.

A legion of formally dressed young people, hauling musical instruments, began mounting the stage. *O,h God no, she's hired an orchestra. How will I get through this? No place to hide.*

As the room quieted, Rabbi Marilyn appeared in a satin robe and skullcap, a gold prayer shawl wrapped around her shoulders. She beckoned us to the *huppa*. Vicky and I faced her, our backs to the seated guests, while Judy and Art stood behind us. Rabbi Marilyn adjusted the little microphone attached to her robe.

"When this couple joined their lives together many years

ago, they each wrote vows and spoke them only to the other. These written vows were then placed in a safe-deposit box in the hope that one day their thoughts would no longer need to be hidden. Today their vows have seen the light of day for the first time in 20 years. Now they will be repeated before all of us assembled."

I could barely speak the words, "I, Joan Denson, do faithfully promise to honor and cherish Vicky Berck, forsaking all others, in sickness and in health, through all adversities, for richer and for poorer till death do us part. I do also promise to give Vicky Berck all the love, respect, understanding and kindness that I possess. I shall share my life with Vicky Berck forever. This is my solemn pledge." *I'm swallowing down tears. Dear God, please don't let my nose drip. I wrote these words so many years ago and still feel the same.*

After Vicky haltingly read from her creased yellow sheet of paper, we exchanged rings. Vicky reached into the tiny pocket of her silk blouse and placed a simple gold band around my finger. I fumbled for its match buried inside my skirt, took her moist hand and gently nudged the gold ring above her knuckle. The rabbi turned away for a moment and came back with two large white handkerchiefs. "Inside are two fragile glasses to remind us of the fragility of life. Life is not to be wasted. Break the goblets and remember!"

We stomped on the glasses at once, causing a loud crunch, and heard the guests yell, "Mazel Tov!" We held each other tightly, as if we were alone in the room.

The orchestra began playing the anniversary waltz. I scurried toward our table, but Vicky gently pulled me back, "Joanie, it's the first dance."

Dancing together in front of everyone? "No, honey, not now."

"If not now, when?"

She took me in her arms, and we waltzed across the floor. I was terrified, but then I saw the faces watching us whirl around the floor; some amused, some with mouths agape, some with proud smiles. After a couple of minutes, even the most stunned trickled onto the dance floor to join us. Only Jerry remained seated, his arms folded across his chest. Couples danced on every side of us, acknowledging our love and theirs—men with women, men with men, women with women—and the worlds that I had struggled all my life to keep apart suddenly converged.

Grateful Acknowledgments

To my partner, Dr. Victoria Berck, for giving me a computer in 1994, against my objections, and telling me to write my story. Vicky was my first and best editor.

***

To my remarkable writing coach, Tristine Rainer, who sent me this note on the day we finished the manuscript:

> Dear Joan,
> It's completed. This has been for me the closest thing to actually living another person's life. I have come to understand things I could not know any other way. And the remarkable thing is, except for the most insignificant difference, you are just like me."
>
> —Tristine

***

To Dr. Janet Smith, my closest friend who read and re-read my scratchings, without complaint. Her confidence and encouragement bouyed me whenever I'd lose hope.

***

To my parents who gave me the freedom to follow my own path. I thank them for giving unswerving support to an often enigmatic daughter.